IN THE NAME OF ALLAH, MOST GRACIOUS, MOST MERCIFUL

CURRENT ISSUES IN ISLAMIC BANKING & FINANCE

DR. SAAD AL-HARRAN

To order additional copies of this book, contact:
Xlibris Corporation
1-888-795-4274
www.Xlibris.com
Orders@Xlibris.com
49566

CONTENTS

DEDICATION

To the souls of my parents who taught me to
share and care for the poor and needy.
May God bless them and have mercy on them.

ACKNOWLEDGEMENT

At the outset, I thank God Almighty for his guidance and courage that He provides me in writing this timely book. This book is a series of short and effective articles written during the last two years on different occasions that reflects the harsh realities the Muslim World is currently passing through as well as the great potentialities it offers for Islamic Banking and Finance institutions in their pursue on social responsibility issues in serving mankind who are under stress and severe pain.

Islam taught me to tell the truth even when it is hard for others to accept because God is with those who said the truth and follow his rightful path to protect society from harm. Today we are living in the age of starvation, hunger, poverty and fear of a deepening then we have moral duty and social responsibility to act and reflect that in writing that is a powerful message that a person can convey to others to wake up whether individuals or institutions before the situation can be out of control.

Islam as a way of life also taught me to give and continue giving to others wherever I go and show to others the beacon of light emanating from the Islamic teachings so that there will be a better future for our children and also humanity when it is facing continuous crisis and there is an urgent need for practical solutions.

I would like to express my thanks and appreciations to Mr. Andrew Morgan, Managing Director and publisher of Redmoney Group, Malaysia who start to publish my various articles on Islamic finance with social responsibility and to his kind editor Mr. Raphael Wong.

My thanks go also to Ms. Cleofe Miranda, Author Service Representative, Xlibris Corporation, USA and Ms. Marianne Baturiano, Asia Printers, Brunei Darussalam for their kind help and assistances.

Last, but not least, my thanks go to my family and especially my daughter, Sarah, who has worked hard in different ways in assisting me in my research projects whom I have taught her with my son Faisal to be responsible to share and care for others and to have a community spirit.

FROM THE AUTHOR

Islamic finance with social responsibility (IFSR) is the new theme of this book. It has been introduced to the general public and is now being promoted by the author through his own writing on Islamic Finance News (*www.islamicfinancenews. com*). I am thankful to its chairman who encourages me to continue writing so those in power in Islamic finance institutions can benefit from my expertise and knowledge in this field. I hope some of my innovative business ideas that I promote in this book will be implemented in order to give hopes to young generation that IFSR is the new vehicle for change for the betterment of mankind in this universe.

The main purpose behind introducing the new concept (IFSR) is the food crisis that hurts the poor and needy badly and has now started to adversely affect a wider segment of societies in Asia, Africa, and Middle East due to soaring food costs and the rise of inflation that may trigger civil unrest in many parts of the Muslim world (MW). The cause's of the surge in food crisis is the massive production of biofuels, which is "a crime against humanity" according to a UN official because of its impact on global food prices that has completely ruined agriculture and will starve millions of people.

Indeed, this concept (IFSR) is timely and overdue and has emerged after twenty-nine years of practical and academic experiences in the field of Islamic banking and finance, during which I have seen some success and many concerns. For the success there are many reasons for that, most of these Islamic finance institutions tend to finance an easy method of operation such as murabahah financing (trade financing) and avoid investment in risk business ventures. For the concerns *mudarahah* and *musharakah* financing (partnership) which are the main methods of financing (which makes them different from others) have been reduced in their operations. It is time to make paradigm shift in the current Islamic finance practices to ease the human suffering due to soaring food prices and cost of living by investing in agriculture farming.

The state of the world today is catastrophic and frightening. Many community leaders are concerned as to where we are heading and if there is any hope in the horizon that safeguards humanity from new conflicts and this time food and water. The conventional financial system is in a state of crisis due to credit crunch in the US mortgage market that is far from over and spread now to some European countries. Their financial market is becoming a market for speculators rather than a market for investors even the skyrocketed oil price exceeding US$140 a barrel was due to speculation, though it is now slipped to less than US$122 but this improvement will not last long. Indeed, such unhealthy world financial environment let to soaring inflation, massive unemployment, recession, armed conflicts and starvation are daily occurrences in many countries that add more suffering to human beings.

The world economic system has to look for structural changes. A plausible option is for Islamic finance with social responsibility to be established at the grassroots level to achieve long-terms social and financial goals in order to establish a just financial system. Its ultimate objectives include the maximization of social capital investment by allocating large sums of funds for human development resources and skills manpower, which Islam promotes. Undoubtedly, Islam focuses on the development of human beings because man is considered to be the vicegerent and active engine for change in the society.

IFSR has duties assigned to it by the Creator of the universe and the real owner of all resources, which will require them to be leaders in the field of finance, management, and strategic marketing to safeguard humanity from exploitation, hatred, and unemployment.

IFSR staff need to be action oriented to understand the importance of the market (Al-Sooq) and to learn from our Prophets (Pbuth) when they used to move round the markets and fully understood what public needs were. Today, the general public needs investment in agriculture to feed people using modern technological innovation such as dripping irrigation to save water, which has started to be a scarce resource in many parts of the Muslim world. We also need investment in applied skills base on hands on experience in order to equip the youth with modern farming practices with innovation by allocating fund for agricultural research and development in order to come up with high-yield seeds for stable crops to feed the citizens of this world.

To achieve that IFSR needs to finance a proposed media campaign entitled **"Time for Change in our lifestyle"** by investing in startup kit to educate the general public about the importance of this new concept and why reducing waste and recycling it are vital for humanity in crisis and to help nature to assist us to safeguard the environment.

This campaign should target affluent societies first in MW where there are too much waste not only in food but also in energy consumption utilizing their food leftovers, mending clothes and energy-saving light bulbs among other initiatives such solar and wind energy investment. Indeed such timely campaign should target the Muslim household in these economies in order to teach them to be disciplined as Islam is not only rituals faith but as a way of life that require us to be responsible and accountable citizens in the planet that need to look after the poor and needy. Our role model is the Prophet Muhammad (Pbuh) who says:

> "None of you truly believes in Allah and in His religion until he
> loves for his brother what he loves for himself".

This hadiths clearly indicates that every member whether in the family, community or society should care for and help one other as Islam teach us to care and share with others humans. The outcome of such media campaign that the author hopes to be published in the newspaper, radio and television and internet should make Muslim family aware that the silent tsunami (food crisis) is with us for many years to come because we have neglecting agriculture investment for three decades because we tend to follow others advice even it is wrong.

Sadly, soaring food prices today causes misery to the public in the MW and radical solutions are urgently needed. I hope these messages from the public can convey one thing that is, Islam is a faith of moderation, anti-waste and for production in order to live a humble life by growing our food in order to feed ourselves first and those unprivileged people second. In doing so we are given direct signals to our children and youth that life is discipline, hard work, sharing and caring and we have to show mercy to others.

These words need to be translated into action by introducing different programs to the community such home gardening scheme (or composting by replicating nature's recycling system) for our children to be supported by IFSR in doing so they will start to appreciate the importance of eating fresh vegetables from their own garden. This experiment is unique because the children will learn how to cultivate fresh vegetables, herbs, or fruits that provide them with a great sense of joy and accomplishment. At the same time it teach them to learn about seed germination, plant growth, flowering, pollination, fruit bearing and ripening — all these miracles are brought home to child gardeners. Indeed, seed sellers report a

40 per cent increase in vegetable seed sales in England as it was recently reported by The Observer British newspaper.

All these initiatives requires funding that I hope will be taken by IFSR headed by Qatar that the author has proposed (please see chapter 11 in this book) entitled *"Can we succeed to make Qatar a role model to the Muslim World"* in order to cement closer relationship between Muslim countries in financial arena as many nations in Asia and Middle East start to be seriously concern about soaring food prices which has become out of control.

Finally, IFSR has a moral duty to invest in renewal energy such as wind and solar and environmental technologies due to the causes of global climate change and what impacts will global warming have on us and our environment. It is time to learn from other nations in climate protection ideas and indeed Germany has made strong headway in this field. The environment industry is booming careers especially in the fields of climate and energy and IFSR has social responsibility to finance modern vocational training institutions in the MW where youth can gain applied skills in rural farming and food processing to enable them to be successful entrepreneurs (after completing their courses successfully) creating wealth and sharing it responsibly in the community.

*All views expressed in this book are entirely personal and do not reflect the opinion of the Faculty of Business, Economics & Policy Studies, Universiti Brunei Darussalam where I work.

Dr. Saad Al-Harran

1st Ramadan 1429   1st September 2008

1 ISLAMIC FINANCE WITH SOCIAL RESPONSIBILITY

The Muslim world is in a stage of crisis financially, economically, and socially; and each day 820 million people in the developing world who mostly are in the Muslim countries do not have enough food to eat or clean water to drink while others are dying in pain due to hunger and starvation. Therefore, food crisis in thirty-six countries, all of which will need extra help, adding to that, poverty and youth unemployment are on the rise and have reached to an alarming level lead to the brink of a social crisis of catastrophic proportions. It has already started in Egypt due to shortages of bread, a life staple for millions of Egyptians, are caused by corruption and soaring prices of unsubsidized bread in the country. For twenty years, the price of one loaf of subsidized bread has been fixed at only five piastres (less than 1cent). The price of unsubsidized bread, however, has steadily risen, reflecting price movement in international markets; and the consequences are far reaching.

These economic and financial crises have come in a critical time where most of the economies of the Muslim world (MW) are in a fragile state due to poor management, oil prices are rocketing exceeding US$147 a barrel last three months. Although it has slipped now below US$120 but this is a temporary recovery as world economy is instable condition due to fallout from sub-prime crisis in US market that has far reaching impact on other financial markets in the western world. This deteriorating situation is a clear indication that food scarcity is an acute problem, especially rice, which is the staple food of half of humanity; but sadly a few nations have rice surpluses, leaving even some of the biggest producers scrambling to grow enough to feed their own people. On the other side of the spectrum, the problem of global warming and world population explosion is plunging humanity into the biggest crisis in human history by pushing up food prices and spreading hunger, starvation, and poverty to a large scale from rural areas into cities.

1

These economic, financial, and social policy failures have come in a time where MW economies have been adversely affected by imposed wars on them by the so-called war on terror with good examples in Iraq, Afghanistan, and Palestine. Adding to that are poor management and lack of strategic planning and investment in new innovative and creative business ideas. Sadly, the MW has not even succeeded to learn from other nations (small country like New Zealand or big country like China) and for instance why a small country in the Pacific like New Zealand (where the author lives permanently) has succeeded in agriculture and farming, food processing, venture capital, and community development and even exporting halal meat while many Muslim nations have food shortages and most of their agriculture produces are imports from abroad.

Chapter 2 highlights the importance of strategic alliances and why they are vital especially for those rich nations in the MW that need help in developing manpower skills and hands-on experiences. Therefore I am of the opinion that Muslim world has entered a critical moment of its survival at the time of food crisis that require Islamic Finance to make a paradigm shift from consumer to produce society to feed the messes and change in the educational curriculum to fulfill market needs for skill manpower that has been discussed in chapter 3.

Similarly to a big nation like China, no real lessons have been learned as to why this populous nation has become number one as global financial power that other nations in the West are concerned about. Surely Prophet Muhammad (Pbuh) is correct when he demanded us to seek knowledge even if it is in China and even if it requires us to travel there.

We should learn from the Chinese how to work hard and why life for them is a struggle while others believe otherwise with the notion that "I will stay in the comfort zone as long as I am happy, and why should I care for others?" Sadly, these kinds of people are self-centered and shortsighted and do things contrary to what Islam wants us, which is to give and share the cakes with others. In Islam, it is always important to give priority to public interest more than individual; that is called *al-maslah al-amah* — to create harmony in the community, not selfishness.

We should also learn from the Chinese about the roots of business success and how they start the business venture at small-scale level using microfinance. It starts when the old family member provides seed capital to his son to begin the journey of life through business-venture struggle, and once he succeeds, he disinvests by withdrawing from business, and the fund goes to the second son. This is what has been called wealth creation and profit distributions. When a

Chinese starts making profit, he makes sure that 90 percent will be reinvested in his business and the rest will be for consumption use, which is contrary with others who mostly consume the profits and borrow money from banks. These values need to be learned from them because China is a producer nation, not consumer, like most of the MW countries today. Even our concept of investment has been manipulated. When they make unproductive investment in high-rise Mega building and hotels, they call it productive. It is time for us to learn from others as life is learning and sharing experience from different cultures and values that have been analysis in chapter 4.

The global halal product industry is a huge business amounting to US$580 billion, yet there is no official authority that looks into the integrity of the halal mark on international market. The rapid development in the industry requires competent and skilled manpower that needs to look at the 4Ps (place, pricing, promotion, and packaging) and build good reputation in the global arena. Once more, this growing industry is fast becoming a new market force, and identifiers need to learn from other nations about the cleanliness aspect and how to handle the meat as well as the storage facilities among other logistic matters. Here New Zealand and Australia have made the headways in these advance industries, and learning from them is a vital component of economic success. Islamic finance has moral responsibility to invest in halal food processing and new product development that has been addressed in chapter 5.

As to the issue of Islamic finance and innovative ideas, it is top priority that needs to be critically addressed by the policy makers as we are in a knowledge-based economy. MW problems are complex to address in a short period of time as it requires structural changes in the economic and financial setting as well as the education system. Today many Muslim thinkers especially those that live in the West are seriously concerned as to which direction the MW education system is leading us and why youth unemployment has reached a crisis level. Does it tell us that rote-learning system of education has paralyzed the minds of our children and youths by not allowing them to be creative and forward thinking and time has come to redesign the curriculum and give more emphasis to practical experiences and vocational training education?

It is time that learning from others needs to be addressed, and Telford Rural Polytechnic (*www.telford.ac.nz*) in New Zealand is a good example that needs to be critically examined as it is considered to be a role model of innovative education and business venture. Telford concept of "A classroom without walls" deserves serious consideration by the policy makers in the MW in order be implemented in our schools and polytechnics.

Telford is New Zealand's only polytechnic that specializes in land-based programs. At this institution students do their very best to gain applied skills and knowledge required for a successful career in the fields of agriculture (sheep, dairy, deer, and beef), equine, forestry, and apiculture (beekeeping). Such unique vocational training has led Telford graduates to find jobs all over the country and the world using the skills and knowledge they first gained while studying on campus.

It is here where Islamic finance with social responsibility (IFSR) should fund rural vocational and technical schools in the MW, such as in Tunisia, Turkey, Syria, Egypt, and Sudan, in order to develop sophisticated and modernized farm industries to combat the food crisis and starvation by achieving self-sufficiency. Such timely investment in human capital should be at Islamic microfinance enterprise level to ensure it is well managed by competent and skilled manpower and incentive system is put in place. I am of the opinion that *musharakah* (partnership financing) and *mudarabah* financing need to be introduced so that the people involved will work hard and understand that life is a struggle in Islam, not a comfort zone that some Muslims believe.

Other mode of financing such as *salam* has also the power to alleviate poverty at the grass roots level in the rural areas of the MW, as it was shown in the recent research conducted by the author (when I was working at the Centre for Islamic Banking, Finance and Management) with my master's students in Islamic banking and finance in September 2007 and now is in the form of a book entitled An Islamic Microfinance Enterprise, The Financial Vehicle That Will Change the Face of the Islamic World: The Power of Salam Financing. It is sale contract whereby the seller undertakes to supply some specific goods to a buyer at a future date in exchange for advanced payment made at the spot. At the time of Prophet Muhammad (Pbuh), this sale was intended to help small farmers or women in handicraft businesses who are struggling hard for cash money to enable them to create demands for their products that will lead to the development of proper line of production which has been addressed in chapter 6 and 7.

The journey of IFSR continues in this world of injustice where global media deceives, lies, and confuses the public because it is their media, not ours, and does not tell us the truth. On the other hand, Islamic finance has a moral duty and responsibility through our media to act and show leadership qualities in the global financial setup that looks for an alternative financial system to show others what Islam is a universal social system that cares for humanity which is in crisis and new wars are looming due to food and water shortages.

The Islamic financial institutions need to face the challenges of today's MW mankind's suffering by offering Islamic microfinance enterprises to ease the daily pain and humiliation done by others in the name of economic development. The world economy today is in deep trouble and recession that puts one hundred million people in low-income countries deeper into poverty and raises the global poverty rate as much as 3 to 5 percentage points according to World Bank senior officer in April 2008.

Indeed in such a critical and depressing time in our history, Islamic finance is on the spotlight and at a crossroad to show strong leadership and be action-oriented institutions that serve a wider community. It is time for Islamic finance to make paradigm shift by investing in human capital and small business ventures not *sukuk* (Islamic bond securities) or capital market that empowers the rich to be richer at the expense of the poor to be poorer. The public need Islamic finance with social responsibility and human capital investment at the grass roots and small farmers in Africa, Asia, and Middle East at microfinance level so people can really benefit from the new social capital institutions.

No doubt, the time is in our side as long as we are prepared to face the challenges and our own global media has a powerful message to convey to the rest of the world that looks for solutions to mankind's suffering from hunger and starvation to youth unemployment that has reached to the highest levels. IFSR needs to be responsible and accountable to educate the public what to do at the time of the human crisis such as food rationing.

The public needs to grow their food at the backyards of their houses; in doing so, we teach our children to be producers, not consumers, if some of us can afford that especially in the affluent Muslim societies where there is too much waste. Alternatively, it is wise to introduce rationing system and adopt a strategy of "thinking of other human beings." Here again, our media needs to teach our children and youths to be responsible and accountable and avoid waste that is unlawful in Islam and can harm humans and the environment. This kind of timely discussion needs to be addressed by the Muslim intellectuals and experienced professionals as to how we can help other humans in Africa, Asia, and Middle East; and the main objective is to come up with plan of action to safeguard the poor and the needy from hunger and starvation looming in the Muslim world.

Luckily with the Qatar leadership of the Sheik Hamad bin Khalifa Al-Thani of Qatar, he realized that the real wealth is not oil and gas, but rather it is competent human capital that needs to be promoted, and the Aljazeera TV channel emerged in 1996 and has worked at great odds in providing an honest and fair assessment to the world of happenings and events. The success of this venture has lead the management in Doha (the capital of Qatar) to open the new Aljazeera International Channel (ALJIC) in 2007 where the headquarters are in Qatar and in different offices in Washington, London, and Kuala Lumpur.

We are of the opinion that MW needs powerful media, and ALJIC can be used an excellent vehicle to promote innovation and creativity. At the same time, Qatar can also play an important role to be the new global Islamic financial hub because of the good work that this small nation has done locally and internationally. Leadership decision of allocating a large sum of oil and Gas revenues in research and development is indeed welcome development. Their important humanitarian roles in the Arab world and far beyond are highly appreciated in assisting their Muslim nations which are in financial stress due to wars or climate changes.

Therefore, the author's view is that Qatar Foundation for Education, Science, and Community needs to strategize with the ALJIC to promote youths with innovative ideas. At the same time ALJIC need to be commercialized innovative research finding internationally through weekly forum to discuss success stories in the MW on innovation and business ventures so as other youths can follow suit while we are in the information age. Here IFSR should support any good business venture even if it is on a small-scale level, and that has been addressed in chapter 8 of the book.

From the above analyses, we should not underestimate the Muslim youth's potentials as they are the engine of change, hope, and economic development. The recent general election in Malaysia on March 2008 has proven that youth votes have played a major role to bring major changes in the political setup in that country. Therefore, IFSR has to listen to them and understand their needs. Regrettably, many youths today are frustrated because they are unemployed, and finding jobs become harder and harder because most of our MW economies are dysfunctional while others are poorly managed. Therefore, IFSR has a moral duty to assist them to be self-employed in any business initiatives that create wealth and share it responsibly in the community and far beyond.

The MW today needs venture capitalists, technologists, entrepreneurs, problem solvers, and hands-on experiences to cultivate our land and feed the starving communities elsewhere whether in Africa, Asia, and Middle East as we are in the age of starvation, hunger, and poverty. Even our education system needs to be radically changed, and more emphasis needs to be focused on the applied sciences and agriculture and farming with Islamic mode of finance put in place to provide incentive and motivation for our youth and school leavers to stay in our rural economies. This has been explained in chapters 9 and 10.

Sadly, many of our high schools and universities in MW students and even lecturers are getting frustrated because of the unsupportive environment that is not conducive to creativity and to think creatively and innovates through discovery knowledge without having to attach themselves to examination demands.

IFSR believes the time has come that our education system needs a paradigm shift from rote learning (that hampers the development of the mind of children and youths to think creatively at primary, intermediate, high school, university, and technical college levels) to "thinking schools" that require students to use their faculty of minds that God Almighty has given to them to use effectively.

Similarly, outdoor activities that many Western schools introduced in their education curriculum setting to allow students to use their imagination and creativity need to be assessed carefully; and if found viable financially by local authorities such as the city council or private businesses, funding of these projects should be catered for. A good example of this is the school composting program in New Zealand schools which attempt to save the environment.

Once more IFSR should target the youth by providing them with funding for any viable new business ideas especially from our schools and polytechnics in order to promote them to be successful entrepreneurs at an earlier level of their education. Indeed, these young innovators are the real wealth of the MW that need to be looked after especially in a knowledge-based global society which we are part and parcel of it so as to create new breed of youth who are venture capitalists and successful entrepreneurs who manage risk and create wealth and then undertake their share of responsibility to the community and far beyond. That requires investment in any intellectual discovery and innovative ideas that will not be realized unless a large sum will be allocated to research and development with the exception of a few countries.

Regrettably, Islamic finance has paid little attention to research and development and investment in new ideas. Some of us don't even appreciate the importance of new ideas that can lead to many scientific discoveries and changes. The later creates a new environment of intellectual excellence, which many of our education institutions are not ready for. In fact, they have missed many good opportunities. It is here where the West has made headway while we are left behind just busy in petty stuff and endless meetings to ascertain why the West

7

has made progress while we have not. Adding to our dilemma is the rote-learning education system that hampers any developmental growth in the mind of our children and youths to think creatively as compared with some other nation like New Zealand, which encourages those with innovative ideas to come forward. It is here where the difference is made by their education system in placing them in a new environment to excel. Innovative and creative students and youths are the real assets of the nation and are considered to be gifted.

Many of us do not appreciate that the world is a global village, and cooperation and collaboration are the norm in the international business, and therefore a small nation cannot survive without strategizing with other nations to utilize their lands and make them ready for cultivation for food security purposes rather than relying on food imports.

At the end, the world is not a safe place any longer; and we are in the age of starvation, hunger, and poverty that trigger riots throughout the globe and fears of a deepening threat to security. While writing this book there are some good sign of hopes that come this time from Qatar. I can expect their leadership to lead the Muslim world because of their wisdom and neutrality in managing and conflicts in the Arab world. Undoubtedly, Qatari leadership has long term vision to unit the MW and I expect them to take the lead in the new concept that I am promoting that is "Islamic finance with social responsibility" make it reality so as Qatar can be considered as role model in the Muslim world. Qatar has made major success not only in global media of AlJazeera but also in the economic and political fronts and the same is also true for quality education and research and development that have been highlighted in chapter 11.

2 WHY STRATEGIC ALLIANCE WITH NEW ZEALAND IS IMPORTANT FOR BRUNEI DARUSSALAM IN MANAGING HER HALAL HUB AND FAR BEYOND INTO THE FUTURE*

We are living in a global village governed by the satellite televisions and the Internet that have connected the Islamic community of 1.5 billion people across the globe with the rest of other human beings. Strategic alliances, venture capitals, and innovative ideas are the lifeblood of the modern business world; and the norms are cooperation, collaborations, and active participation in any business ventures to enable a small nation to move forward and survive by sharing their thoughts and concern with other nations.

Undoubtedly, small nations and communities can't survive today by themselves in a highly complex, globally competitive environment unless they have to cooperate and strategize their citizens mentally and emotionally and prepare them to face the challenges of the twenty-first century. Small nations have to work hard and appreciate the importance of time and managing business risks effectively by collaborating with other nations and sharing ideas and intellectual thoughts across cultures in order to succeed in this worldly life and create wealth and share it among their citizens.

This requires strategic thinking and dynamic processes that allow changes to take place and thus creating a conducive environment to support it. This process requires development of new skills to empower the young generation so that they can be equipped to be employable and successful entrepreneurs and effectively utilize the natural resources that God Almighty has given to a small nation. The same is also true among individuals or groups of people or communities to cooperate and collaborate to see what other communities can provide.

9

This paper will highlight the importance of the strategic alliance. It will also discuss two important concepts that deserve serious attention by the policy makers in Brunei Darussalam — that is, *Ta'aroof* (knowing each other) and *Ta'aawun* (cooperating) with other human beings what these concepts can lead to. The issue of what New Zealand can offer to Brunei not only in managing her halal hub but far beyond has been assessed. Issues such as skilled manpower training, successful history of innovation, sound industrial and agricultural bases, ecotourism, and new culture of adventure have been examined. Finally policy recommendations have been suggested in order to be examined by the policy makers in Brunei Darussalam Ministry of Industry and Primary Resources and in New Zealand, which is keen to assist in different ways.

1. Introduction

"Strategic alliance" (SA) can be defined as a cooperative development of successful, long-term, strategic relationships based on mutual trust, world-class and sustainable competitive advantage for all the partners, relationships which have a further separate and positive impact outside the partnership or alliance (Lendrum). An alliance can involve joint research efforts, technology sharing, joint use of production facilities, marketing of one another's products, or the joining of forces to manufacture components or assemble finished products (Theompson, A. A., and Stirckland, A. J.).

It is also defined as any relationship between companies involving a sharing of common destinies; strategic alliance is cropping up across the global arena. Due to the maturation of several trends of the 1980's, such as intensified foreign competition, shortened product life cycles, soaring cost of capital, including the cost of research and development, and ever-growing demand for new technologies, alliance is becoming an attractive strategy for the future (Al-Harran, S.).

2. Does Islam encourage us to do *Ta'aroof* (knowing each other) and *Ta'aawun* (cooperation) with other human beings?

Islam is a faith of *Ta'aroof* (knowing each other) and *Ta'aawun* (cooperation) with other human beings in matters of righteousness to God or benefit to humanity to enable mankind to live in peace and harmony with others. This relationship is vital in the world of today that is governed by wars (in the Middle East, Asia, and Africa) hunger, starvation, and environmental crisis that lead many people to ask, where are we heading?

Allah Almighty says:

> O mankind! We created you from single (pair) of a male and a female, and made you into Nations and tribes, that ye may know each other (Not that ye may despise Each other. Verily the most honored of you in the sight of God is (he who is the most Righteous of you). (Sura Al-Hujurat 13)

> Help you one another in charity and piety, but help you not one another in sin and rancor: fear Allah for Allah is severe in punishment. (Sura Al-Miada 2)

These two clauses clearly state that God Almighty wants all mankind whether Muslims or non-Muslims to know each other first and to cooperate with each

11

other second in righteous ways to cement closer relationship between one nation to another and one tribe with another. What makes a relationship continue is mutual trust, respect of one culture to another, hard work, and learning from each other to achieve economic prosperity to all mankind.

Human societies and communities need to cooperate to survive, and if avenues of good and righteous cooperation are closed and this virtue is not nurtured in the individuals, people turn to cooperation in sin (*Al-ithm Wal Udwan*) and enmity such as bribery, nepotism, and other forms of corruption. Indeed, cooperate in good things and cooperate not in evil with non-Muslims (Anjum U.).

It is also notable that the second verse of the Quran commands us to cooperate in acts or matters of goodness rather than with good or believing people. It invites us to focus on what to cooperate on, not with whom to cooperate. It is so because the concept of cooperation is general and inclusive of all human beings — one does not have to share their beliefs, cultures, or ideologies in order to cooperate with them. The only requirement is that the shared objective be good.

3. What does *Ta'aroof* (knowing each other) and *Ta'aawun* (cooperation) lead us to?

Brunei Darussalam is a small state with a population of about 380,000. It is a blessed nation with abundant natural resources that require effective utilization of these valuable assets for the benefit of the community. Islam is a dynamic faith that encourages us to work hard and to struggle for the success (*Falah*) in this life and the hereafter. Then the concept of *Amal* (work) and the conduct of it must also be efficient (*Eteekan*) and effective to drive the economy forward, creating wealth and sharing it responsibly in the community.

Therefore, work and efficiency of *Amal* (work) are complementing each other. Islam wants us to be a producer and not a consumer society since God Almighty has given us his endless bounties *(Taskhyeer)* from fertile lands to rivers, seas, and oceans and a beautiful sunny environment ready for farming and agriculture, forestry, fishery, and agribusiness in order to achieve self-sufficiency in food security for ourselves and others in need with cooperation with others (Low, 2007).

Undoubtedly, it is through *Ta'aroof* and *Ta'aawun* that the following aims will be realized:

> Bruneian economy will grow; and new business opportunities
> will emerge starting from utilization of farming and agriculture

in the country, which has been shrinking steadily over the past couple of years (*www.brudirect.com*), by establishing agribusiness and joint ventures with new business partners.

1. Improvement in economic performance of the country gives further support to the government under the leadership of His Majesty the Sultan; who has often stressed the importance of small business enterprises because he is keen to see this sector of the economy growing since these two resources (oil and gas) will not last forever. In doing so, diversifying the economy (through time) will lead to lessening dependence on oil and gas.

2. Manpower training of young graduates whether in universities or institutions of high learning is a vital component for the growing economy. To achieve that, those young graduates will have high hopes and expectations to excel in the business world once they will be given the opportunities after obtaining practical skills that the market needs. Undoubtedly, young graduates are the engine of economic development and prosperity of each nation. They need to be effectively utilized as graduates today are looking for business ventures to face the challenges; that will not be realized unless they will be equipped with modern applied skills in farming technologies, graphic design, mass media and journalism, tourism and hospitality, marine life, and sports.

3. Cooperation between universities and vocational training institutions in the field of applied sciences and business ventures. Exchange programs will enhance universities to know and learn from other institutions in the area of research and development. Telford Rural Polytechnic, Balclutha, New Zealand (*www.telford.ac.nz*), is a world-class college that specializes in practical rural training in agriculture, apiculture, equine studies, and forestry. It is indeed an excellent example of empowerment of the young some of whom are successful entrepreneurs serving the community and nation.

3. What can New Zealand offer to Brunei Darussalam?

Before we discuss what a small nation in the Pacific can offer to her counterpart in Southeast Asia, it is fair to give a brief background about New Zealand.

New Zealand is a country in the southwestern Pacific Ocean comprising two large islands (the North Island and the South Island) and numerous small islands, most notably Stewart Island and the Chatham Islands. In Maori, New Zealand has come to be known as Aotearoa which is usually translated into English as the land of the long white cloud.

The New Zealand's population is estimated to be 4,184,600 in 2006 (Statistics New Zealand) which is mostly of European descent, with the indigenous Maori being the largest minority. Non-Maori Polynesian and Asian people are also significant minorities, especially in the cities. Elizabeth II, as the queen of New Zealand, is the head of state and in her absence is represented by a non-Partisan governor-general. Political power is held by the democratically-elected parliament of New Zealand under the leadership of the prime minister who is the head of government.

New Zealand was granted limited self-government in the 1850s and by the late nineteenth century was a fully self-governing country in most senses. In 1893, it became the first nation in the world to grant women the right to vote. In 1907, New Zealand became an independent Dominion and a fully independent nation in 1947 when the Statute of Westminster (1931) was ratified, although in practice Britain had ceased to play any real role in the government of New Zealand much earlier than this. As New Zealand became more politically independent, it became dependent economically; in the 1980s, refrigerated shipping allowed New Zealand to base its entire economy on the export of meat and dairy products to Britain.

Economy

New Zealand's economy is relatively small and has been a strong performer in the last decade, compares well by international standards (*www.newzealandnow. info*). The economy has continued on its strong upward course, and living standards—measured as real GDP per person—have risen steadily over the past decade, putting the country on track towards the government's objective of returning to the top half of the Organization for Economic Co-operation and Development (OECD). But capacity has become increasingly strained, and monetary policy has been tightened to ensure inflation remains well anchored. The country's prospects are bright, with potential growth projected to remain comfortably above 3% per year over the medium term.

As of June 2005, New Zealand's unemployment rate had dropped to 3.7 percent—the lowest in the developed world. While employment growth rate has been impressive, labor productivity growth of 1.5 percent a year over the last five years is lower than the OECD average. Lifting labor productivity is now the central challenge for the country to generate long-term sustainable economic growth and return the economy output to the top half of the OECD. The country has historical strengths in the primary sector as well as more recently in tourism.

Halal Integrity

New Zealand prides itself on meeting the religious requirements of its Muslim customers. Beef from New Zealand that is certified halal has been slaughtered in accordance with the Islamic Shariah using humane and hygienic techniques. The Federation of Islamic Associations of New Zealand (FIANZ) halal certification has played a vital role in the development of markets for New Zealand beef and sheep meat in the halal markets (countries with majority Muslim population) (Farouk, M.). The proportion of New Zealand's annual meat exports, which go to halal markets, stands currently at 9.7 percent and 8.4 percent for sheep meat and beef, respectively. This represents a significant share of the global trade in halal sheep meat. Other authorized company which does certification is New Zealand Islamic Meat Management (NZIMM). FIANZ has been certifying meat as halal since the mid-1980s while NZIMM has been certifying meat since the halal trade from New Zealand began.

As to the issue of halal certification, the following requirements must be met before a halal slaughter certificate is issued,

a. All cattle are clean and rested prior to walking to the slaughter zone.

b. Slaughtering is carried out by a practicing Muslim who must be mentally stable and proven in his principles and general knowledge of Islam, having been recommended by his mosque and closely questioned at the time of the recruiting interview (*www.newzealandbeef.org*).

c. Animals are electrically stunned (nonfatally) and slaughtered promptly out of the sight of other animals. Halal supervisors routinely test animals to ensure they are only made temporarily unconscious by the stunning and are alive when they are slaughtered, as required by Islamic law.

d. While slaughtering the animal, the slaughter man recites "In the name of Allah, the Most Gracious, the Most Merciful" while facing the direction of the House of Allah (*Al-Kaabah Al-Sharifah*).

e. The knife used for slaughtering is razor sharp, and the cutting is done in one go.

15

f.   The cut quickly severs the respiratory passage, jugular veins, carotid arteries, and esophagus; but the spinal cord is intact. This ensures the complete draining of blood and a quick death.

If an animal is not slaughtered in the above manner, it is non-halal. The certifying authorities and the processing company's total quality management program ensure compliance with these requirements.

Halal meat and storage is completely separate from any meat that is declared non-halal by the Muslim slaughter man or halal-certifying authority. These requirements are enforced by halal-certifying authorities at all approved halal processing and packaging houses throughout New Zealand.

Brunei Management of Halal Hub

Brunei has entered the global halal meat business because she sees it has great business potential in the future to serve not only local but also regional and international market as well as Muslims and non-Muslim customers. The global halal market (similar to Islamic finance) is US$600 billon per annum and has become and has become highly competitive business ventures with many competitors in the global market. Therefore, the industry requires sound foundation in terms of skilled manpower and expertise in the field of strategic marketing and handling the meat and storing it in the right places. The hygienic issues and cleanliness of the places (markets) are also vitally important because we are dealing with a global product, and the customers who eat the meats are health conscious that what they eat are of top quality at a competitive price. Therefore, the arts of staying in the global market today are innovation, competition, and competent manpower in order to create competitive advantage in the global economy.

Brunei is aiming to be a global player in the premium halal market. It will launch its coveted Brunei Premium Halal Brand, setting its sights to become one of the major players of the halal brand globally. No doubt, it is an interesting development as it is a niche market for Brunei according to Permanent Secretary of the Ministry of Industry and Primary Resources (MIPR) Dato Hamid Jaafar (*Asia Inc*, July — August 2007).

The Brunei government is supporting the Premium Halal Brand project; and various ministries such as Ministry of Industry and Primary Resources (MIPR), Brunei Islamic Religious Council, and the Ministry of Health are giving their blessing for the timely initiative.

Australia's Elders Victoria is coordinating with Brunei Darussalam halal brand to develop global premium halal products by the middle of next year (Izam, S., and Shareen Han, *The Brunei Times*).

We are of the opinion that the policy makers are keen to see this good initiative succeed in the global market by having sound foundation, efficient management, and what other nation can offer. New Zealand can assist Brunei by becoming a strategic partner in order to succeed in the halal meat market throughout the world and far beyond. The areas of business interest that Brunei needs to explore with New Zealand are the following:

a. Skilled Manpower Training

The knowledge economy today is governed by skilled and competent manpower, creativity, innovation, and excellence. Undoubtedly, each nation is raising its education standard of excellence in technical skills through competency by generating greater public awareness and interest in technical education. The key message for each nation is they have to develop talent for global needs. Singapore is a good example in doing that through its Institute of Technical Education (ITE), and school reform is already under way to prepare its youth to face the future challenges. These changes have been progressive ones in that they are aimed at accomplishing two goals crucial in education: offering a variety of choices to suit aptitudes and interests and steering talents to the appropriate disciplines so that no waste results (*The Straits Times*, 2007).

We believe vocational training institutions and polytechnics are the answer to skilled manpower concern in Brunei, and New Zealand can assist in providing tailor-made twinning program with Christchurch Polytechnic Institute of Technology (*www.cpit.ac.nz*) to alleviate youth unemployment which has reached a level of 7.3 percent in 2006 according to Research and Planning Division, Labor Department, Brunei Darussalam (Yussof, A.).

Applied courses such as certificate in pre-trade plumbing, gas fitting, and drain laying; fitness instructing; and building trading are of great demands in the global market. According to the study conducted by Varina Nissen, managing director, Manpower Australia (*www.manpower.com.au*) the top-earning jobs in 2020 (annual salaries of workers, excluding management and executive) are:

Plumbers – $148,000
Fitness instructors – $147,876
Building traders – $140,225
IT workers – $128,298$

b. A Success Story in Innovation as Learned from Canterbury University

The world has become a global village where one nation learns from others. It is time for Brunei Darussalam to assess and examine some successful stories in business ventures in the Pacific such as New Zealand. Why are micro strategic alliances between science and engineering colleges and business schools vital for Brunei in the information age? For instance, a small company called Canterprise, the arm of Canterbury University, Christchurch, New Zealand (*www.cant.canterbury.ac.nz*), has made several successes with innovative new companies simply because it turns good ideas into saleable and profitable products and services. Today, Canterprise has spun off companies such as WhisperTech, which has a $300 million order for its innovative domestic heating units; chemical sniffer technology company Syft Technologies; and Veritde, which is developing a handheld device to detect anthrax and other bioterrorism threats (Marta, Steeman 2007).

c. Sound Industrial and Agricultural Base

Individuals have been given many gifts by the Creator God Almighty; and the most important one is the faculty of mind, wisdom, responsibility, and accountability to utilize the land (*Esteemar*) in order to achieve modernity and prosperity density. The same is also true for nations that the Creator has given endless natural resources. The minds of mankind can be combined with these assets to achieve sound economic development inspirits civilizations that are the main focus for the development of human beings.

The Holy Quran has used it to open our minds to face the challenges.

> We sent down Iron, in which is material for mighty was, as well as many benefits for mankind, that God may test who it is that will help. (Sura Iron 25)

The concept of sending down Iron from God Almighty's universe has a powerful message to mankind – that is, industrialization is vital for human civilization and the nation's prosperity (Al-Rashed, M. A.). Therefore, building sound industrial base is a must for any nation to achieve economic development with three ingredients of the success in our minds; and these are commandments of protecting good and forbidding evil, justice which gives to each person his due, and the strong arm of the law, which maintains sanctions for evil doers (Yusuf Ali).

Similarly, water was sent down from the clouds in abundance so that the nation could achieve agricultural development and food security.

Here again the Quran says:

> And do we not send down from the clouds water in abundance, That We may produce Therewith corn and vegetables and gardens of luxurious growth. (Sura Nabaa 14-16)

Therefore, industrialization and agricultural development (IGD) go hand in hand, and in the case of small nations like Brunei, it should start as micro IGD small-scale level with sound foundation, and New Zealand can assist Bruneian youths in applied skills in order to see them as successful entrepreneurs. Islamic banks here have moral duty to assist youths to excel as finance is human rights in Islam.

d.   **Ecotourism and Adventure Tourism (Sharing the Experiences)**

Ecotourism is very popular internationally, and New Zealand is in a unique position to capitalize on its spectacular scenery and native flora and fauna, which Brunei is good at as well, and there is always room for sharing the experience between the two nations. In addition to New Zealand's outdoor adventure activities, it also offers excursions that ensure you get to see some of the beautiful, less traveled parts of the countryside — enjoy the taste of New Zealand ecotourism and relish the rush of the New Zealand adventure tourism scene.

Whether its bird life, the whales, seals, and dolphins or just the tranquility of New Zealand's unspoiled outdoors, tourists will find richness and diversity always close to the doorstep in New Zealand. Ecotourism is New Zealand's way of showing off to the world the natural beauty of the country's wild places. New Zealand is famous for bungee jumping, which is certainly adventure tourism that most people like.

e.   **New Culture of Venture Capitalists and Entrepreneurs**

New Zealand is known internationally as an adventurer's nation with a hands-on experience, and Sir Edmund Hillary is a unique personality in the history of the country that inspired many people including the youth. He conquered Mount Everest and the South Pole and captured the world's imagination. He said,

> I have modest abilities, I combine these with a good deal of determination and I rather like to succeed.

I believe Sir Edmund is correct because it is through human efforts, long-term vision, maintaining focus, and determination that success will be achieved (*www.nzedge.com/heroes/hillary.html*). It is this message that the Government of His Majesty the Sultan wants to convey to the young Bruneians that state jobs are no longer secured and time has come to venture to business and innovation. To achieve that, the government needs to create the climate for the young generation to succeed locally and internationally.

f.   Another Success Story of Community Hospital in Christchurch

Health is the real wealth of humans in this life. It is through a good health system, quest for knowledge continues.

Indeed, it is community spirit through cooperation and coordination in terms of raising funds that Christchurch, the Garden City of New Zealand, has succeeded to establish high tech community hospital to serve the community. This interesting experience needs to be studied carefully in order to be replicated in Brunei so the children and youths will appreciate the importance of community and the concept of giving and helping others (The Canterbury Community Trust).

Conclusions and Recommendations

The author's paper is practical and has policy implications. It has been written based on the author's long experience in the field of Islamic finance and work with youth entrepreneurs. The suggestions made need to be critically examined by the policy makers of the Ministry of Industry and Primary Resources and practitioners and successful business leaders in order to form a strategic committee to assess each items proposed in the paper in order to come up with an plan of action.

Although New Zealand is a small country in terms of its population, the state is an innovative and enterprising nation. It is a well-respected nation in the global arena because of its hardworking citizens, honesty, dignity, and business excellence. Farming, food processing, and halal meat production and handling have made New Zealand succeed in the global market; and it is keen to share its experience and assist other small nations like Brunei Darussalam to make progress in the world arena. Brunei, on the other hand, as a small nation, is facing many challenges. Learning from other nation's experiences in applied skills, new ideas (Al-Harran, S.), and work ethics are vitally important in order to see the economy growing and prospering; and that is what the leadership is looking for.

* *Paper presented at the International Conference on Business and Management on Creating Competitive Advantage in the Global Economy, Organized by the Faculty of Business, Economics, and Policy Studies, Universiti Brunei Darussalam (UBD), 8-9 January 2008, Brunei Darussalam.*

3 TIME FOR PARADIGM SHIFT: WHAT ISLAMIC FINANCE WITH SOCIAL RESPONSIBILITY (IFSR) CAN DO AT THE TIME OF HUMAN CRISIS

The Muslim World (MW) has entered a new era of financial instability, weakening economic system, social upheaval and civil unrest looming in different parts of the developing countries and even developed nations. Indeed, the recent incident in South Africa where locals have killed savagely other humans from Zimbabwe and Somalia (who escaped civil war and move to other nation for peace and seeking employment) due to false allegations that they took their jobs, give us clear indication how serious food crisis really is and what impacts soaring food costs on the poor and the needy.

Surely, these events are going to be common in terms of its occurrence and magnitude in the world of injustice and greediness by a few individuals or corporations. Thanks to those in power who spend billion of dollars for alternative energy such as biofuel or biodiesal that have made the price of rice and wheat sky rocketing because it is the main staple food for millions of people in Asia, Africa and Middle East. Sadly, rice and wheat have now entered the global casino market so-called "the stock market" and those food items are under a new game that is called "food speculation". One can wonder who benefits most from food price hikes, surely the speculators and the rich who can afford to pay high prices for purchasing top quality of rice and wheat for instant gratification at the expense of the underprivileged that can't.

At the same time, the powerful nations have encouraged their own farmers through government subsidies and cheap credit to grow maize, soybean, corn and palm oil to generate alternative source of energy to increase their wealth at the same time have more control on other nations (that are already variable due to impose wars, dysfunctional economies and widespread corruption) and this time through rice and wheat as strategic staple food crops.

The strategic plan is obvious to further weakening MW governments by powerful nations so they are ready for new occupations or they can create civil unrest to them and Sudan is good example and Darfur region which is full of natural resources mainly oil. These governments are no longer can afford to fund subsidies to their own citizens due to the fiscal and financial constraints and balance of payment crisis due to world wide recession. These events will surely trigger civil war between nations either internally through civil unrest that start to gain momentum in many parts of the MW and the worse is yet to come. Indeed, we are not in the age of human catastrophe that has no limits nor boundaries to control that will put Islamic finance on the headline news as what these institutions can do to defuse tension. Therefore, Islamic Finance with social responsibility has a moral duty to act before it get worse day after day that require intervention through investment in Islamic microfinance projects to safeguard humanity from new food crisis Tsunami that affect billion of people in this plant.

The paradigm shift from consumer to producer society

Undoubtedly, most of the MW economies are consumer and not producers societies and therefore we are variable to the world market fluctuations in food supply items mainly rice and wheat. Basically these harsh realities of our economies have always made us rely on others especially the powerful nations to feed our citizens and naturally we are weak and not ready for crisis of that magnitude. Regrettably even in some of affluent economies they tend to take life easy as a comfort zone and never utilize their fertile lands that Allah Almighty has given to them. The general tendency among the public is as long as food is coming to us from abroad or from the neighboring countries why should we worry but the hard question is for how long they will continue to do that without understanding the impact of such an attitude or mindset.

Sadly, most MW economies have become nations of dependent on others to feed us that have made us weak and fragile because we have neglected the basic needs of human survival that is food and water for more than three decades. Such short sighted attitudes need to be changed now and we have to be ready to be a producer society respected among other nations and be blessed by the Allah Almighty so we can feed our self rather than to be fed by others. That will lead to job creations and youth unemployment reduction.

From the above scenario, I can say the solution is in our hands and our wills that is production through farming and rice plantation. Indeed, farming is the dignity of human beings through which farmers produce their own crops, feed their own family and children and sale the produce in the local market at lower prices. Although profit margins were relatively low at the time of harvesting of the crops, farmers were happier because they brought fresh food to their homes and feed their families and share it with relatives and neighbors.

One of the leading Islamic bank in rural development, Sudanese Islamic Bank (SIB) has discovered that farmers were exploited by the money lenders the *shail* merchant who charges exorbitant interest rates along with other factors such as the failure of the organized credit markets to assist them. Therefore, the management of SIB has decided to enter the farming business and become as strategic partner to the small farmers that helped them immensely base on profit and loss sharing system (*musharakah*). That has worked well for the two parties' base on that SIB started to provide fixed assets such as tractors, ploughs, harrows, water pumps and inputs such as seeds, fertilizers, pesticides, fuel, jute sacks and co-management, marketing, storing and extension. The farmer on the other hand contributes with his land, labour, part of the running expenses and management. From the net profit the farmer gets 30% for management. The remaining profit 70% is divided between SIB and the farmer according to their equity share.

Similarly *Salam* financing, the needs of the small farmers were met by providing money needed to grow their crops and to feed their family up to the time of harvest has great potentials. These two contracts of profit-loss-sharing and *Salam* contracts with sound and efficient management put in place are the main solutions to our current food crisis. Bearing in mind *Aljazeera* lands in Sudan are fertile and a good place for cultivation of rice.

What IFSR Can Do?

Islam is social security system that looks after the poor and the needy. Wealth in Islam has a social responsibility role because it has been given by the God Almighty to individuals, institutions or nations as a test to see whether it has been effectively utilized or it is been concentrated by the hand of few. If it is the latter then there will be no peace and security in this world. Islam has institutionalized *Zakat* and *Sadakat* to achieve social justice and create harmony and loving and caring for mankind that will also applied for societies or nations that most of the MW are missing due to exploitation of the rich to the poor, corruption and imposed wars to add more suffering to humans in Iraq, Palestine and Afghanistan.

Therefore, IFSR has moral and social responsibility to support any new initiatives such as seed capital for Muslim scientists to come up with new agriculture innovation or interest free loan to help the small farmers to start paddy plantation in Morocco, Tunisia, Sudan and Indonesia with less government intervention. Surely these initiatives if it will plan and well managed it can bring fruitful result by creating food security zone in the MW. Similarly building food silos to keep rice and wheat for longer period is also important that need to be supported by IFSR.

How IFSR Can Achieve Food Security?

Training is the first point to change our mindset and attitude towards agriculture and rural development. It should start with rice plantation and rural farming skills that equip Muslim youth to be active business partners with IFSR that require the later to provide credit, interest free loan or scholarship for any youth who want to venture in rural farming course. This requires IFSR to contact the following institutions International Rice Research Institute in Manila, Philippine (*www. training.irri.org*) and Telford Rural Polytechnic in New Zealand (*www.telford. ac.nz*) seeking their help and assistance in this highly demand area of expertise which most MW economies are lacking.

For the former institution IRRI in Philippine its aim is to improve the understanding of new scientists, development professionals, and others on the importance of rice and its production methods. This institution conduct courses because rice is Asia's most economically and culturally important food crop and its production is regarded as the single most important economic activity on the planet. Similarly to the Middle East and Africa nations rice is an important staple food that no family can afford to miss.

Indeed, at the time of food crisis in MW course of that nature is vitally important because it enable the participant to:

1) Appreciate the importance of rice and the environment where rice is being grown.
2) Understand how rice varieties are developed and how seed is produced.
3) Recognize and apply the important techniques of rice culture
4) Detect, identify and solve common field problems of rice production.
5) Perform field operations in rice culture.

Indeed such unique course is of great demands in the market place. Here I proposed that MW governments can go to production line such as rice and wheat by using modern methods of rice plant that is morphology of the rice plant, growth stages of the rice plant and races and plant types. Here were IFSR can assist financially by make cooperation with IRRI training to train Muslim youth. In today youth unemployment is huge burden on the most governments in the MW that course is a great applied asset that equips them with modern scientific methods and new technological methods in rice plant.

While the later that is Telford Rural Polytechnic in Balclutha, New Zealand that provide students with modern skills and knowledge required for a successful career in the fields of Agriculture farming such as (Sheep, Dairy, Deer & Beef), Equine, Forestry and Apiculture (Beekeeping).

I am of the opinion that these two applied courses are significantly important that requires us to propose another paradigm shift that is NW educational curriculum. Sadly most of the tertiary institutions in the MW are dysfunctional due to lack of financial support from the governments, poor managerial leadership and outdated curriculums that make our youth get bored when they go every day to study because the teaching methods are purely theoretical with no practical experiences. Students get lost with so many theories most of which are not applicable because it was copies from the powerful nations and can't apply in the MW economies.

It is time to change the curriculum in MW institutions of high learning and more emphasis should be given to applied science. A course such us Islamic Microfinance Enterprises should be introduced in every universities and polytechnics in the MW that gives more weight to the application let say (70%) and the remaining (30%) on the theories. Here again IFSR has to promote this initiatives by proposing changing of our curriculum to the ministries of Education and Institutions of high learning.

Food crisis is complex issue to tackle as it requires change in the mindset, attitude of people in power in the MW towards life and strategic planning and learning from others nations and cultures. I am of the opinion that time has come to move to farming and rice production with modern skills and knowledge that what most of the MW governments urgently needed. Now we should reply on themselves as Allah almighty has given the Muslim world abundant of natural resources that need competent and skill manpower to utilize it effectively.

Finally, the wealth of Islamic banks continue growing at 15 percent in each of the past three years, with global volumes at $97.3 billion by the end of last year according to international credit rating agency Moody's in midst of poverty and hunger and starvation and now food crisis. But sadly mostly of these funds were invested in hardware Mega buildings or expensive hotels that will not benefit the ordinary people but only the rich and affluent citizens and time has come for paradigm shift to face the reality of the Muslim world. How far Islamic finance will succeed to make the paradigm shift time and history will tell.

4 THE ROOTS OF CHINESE BUSINESS SUCCESS

Although the global economy is in a recession due to the turmoil stemming from credit crisis in the **United States** as well as housing market meltdown, the news from Societe Generale about the brokerage fraud that shocked the world and Swiss banking giant UBS announced a full-year loss of US$3.5 billion and others to come as the fallout occurring elsewhere.

Even when a gloomy picture predicated for the world economy, people today are enjoying buying goods and services for instant gratification while others are rushing to the shopping malls to purchase commodities either because they are on special offer or because they are discounted, things that businesses provide to their customers during the festive session, such as Chinese New Year that started on 7 February 2008.

Indeed, shopping malls are busier where it is full of people enjoying last-minute shopping. The mall is now considered an entertainment and fun place where the consumer citizens of the world are enjoying having fast food from McDonald's or KFC. Children are busy eating their hamburgers and at the same time rushing to play computer games such as Time Out for fun, but in reality we teach them how to be violent to other humans and to the environment.

Naturally, Chinese entrepreneurs are making use of global markets whether in New York, London, Malaysia, Hong Kong, or New Zealand by decorating their malls and main high streets in beautiful colors that attract our attention and take us to a different world of endless desires. Indeed, going to shopping malls today is a memorable experience in our lives especially for our wives and teenagers. Surely, these successful entrepreneurs are also enjoying good profit during this festival period, thanks to the credit card industries that make our lives easier and instantaneous. This inculcates a habit of spending beyond our means that has become the norm and blatant carelessness for debt accumulation as long as we have instant gratification.

Many of us are asking questions: What are the roots of Chinese business success in the global market? Is it really the Chinese culture that teaches them how to manage business venture risks successfully and drive them to work harder? Or is it the environment that allows them to succeed wherever they land or the seed capital provided by their fathers or grandfathers to enable their young sons to start their business ventures or a combination of all these ingredients which make their success very unique?

If this assessment is correct, then we can now realize why Prophet Muhammad (Pbuh) said:

Seek knowledge even if it is in China and even if it requires you to travel there.

This Hadith has strategic marketing significance, which many of us underestimate. Surely the Prophet is correct, and we should learn from the Chinese how they run business and how they manage risks and why family finance is far better than bank borrowing and why savings are important to be reinvested rather than be consumed.

Undoubtedly, all of these analyses have highlighted the main ingredients of Chinese business success today though the social costs are also high where poverty in the rural areas is also on the rise. But no doubt, China today is the number one financial superpower in the global market arena, and many advanced worlds are watching where the Chinese empire goes to.

But let's go back to the roots of the Chinese success in understanding the concept of finance. It is similar to Islamic microfinance, which is a financing tool that provides very small loans to the working underprivileged people who are traditionally considered as non-bankable, mainly because they lack the guarantees that can protect a financial institution against a loss. Furthermore, Islamic microfinance provides an innovative interest-free alternative to conventional microfinance. Based on the profit-sharing principles of equity-based finance, it also offers greater resilience than conventional microfinance. If a business fails, nothing is paid; if a business succeeds, profits are shared. Risks and rewards are always proportionate to equity shares.

Here a Chinese father provides interest-free loan to his young son or equity financing in the business ventures including advising him to look after the fund and utilizing it effectively and efficiently in order to succeed. Here the message from father to son is valuable in that it reflect his wisdom, his knowledge, and his understanding of the market. Once the business succeeds and generates profit, the father through diminishing partnership concept this will ensure whatever profit he has made can move to the other sons. Here the wealth is circulated from the first son to other siblings.

That reminds me of my teaching experience in International Islamic University Malaysia (1991-1996). One Chinese student came to my office, and through our conversation, I asked her what her concept of life is. She replied, "Sir, it is a life struggle, and I must succeed either in the university or in the business world."

What does this statement tell us?

1. That she is determined and that she must succeed. This is what business is all about: hard work, (sweating), struggle for survival, and creating wealth.

2. The concept of hard work is similar to what Quran (*Kadah*) wants us to adopt, meaning toiling until death. Here Allah says:

    > Thou man Verily thou art ever Toiling on towards thy Lord Painfully toiling, but thou shalt meet Him. (Sura Inshiqaq 4-6)

3. How many of us are taking life as a struggle? Regrettably very few and this is why we have endless problems. Sadly, many of us consider life is a comfort zone, and as long as I am happy with my family and children, why should I care for others?

4. The concept of *I* and *we* need to be re-examined. We are after all one family with different cultures and values, and if one part is affected, surely the rest will be affected also.

5 MARKETING OF HALAL PRODUCTS: THE WAY FORWARD*

Today, Islam is the fastest-growing religion on earth, both by birth and adoption, with the Muslim population estimated to reach 2 billion by 2010. With the global halal market estimated to be worth US$580 billion a year and the halal food industry pegged to grow at a rate of 7 percent annually (*Asia Inc*, July-August 2007), businesses should indeed be tapping at this growing market segment.

Halal's burgeoning popularity can be linked to religious fervor and beliefs that it's cleaner, healthier, and tastier (Burgmann 2007). Halal logo has now become a symbol of quality and religious compliance, and this makes it sound as the new green. Then again, some argue it is driven by consumers' urge to follow a ritual or their desire for acceptance while others see it as part and parcel of another rising global trend.

Another reason for the tremendous acceptance of halal within the global population is the process of assimilation. Foreign foods in some countries as in Europe have become assimilated, and local tastes are changing, encouraged by global tourism and reverse colonization. Curry is now the number one takeaway meal in the United Kingdom, and kebabs are a typical German staple (Evans 2007).

Halal has also been subjected to different interpretations to include other nonfood segments. Most broadly, it may also be applied to cosmetics and pharmaceuticals, hygiene products and nutritional supplements, travel, art, music, and books—even marriage and finance (Burgmann 2007).

Emphasis on halal is also growing. It is fast becoming a new market force and identifier and is now moving into the mainstream market, affecting and changing perception on how businesses are being conducted, including from a marketing point of view.

The Marketing of Halal Products

The study of consumer behavior is vital when it comes to marketing of halal products. The fact of the matter is, Muslim consumers are very much similar to any other consumer segments, demanding healthy and quality products, which must also conform to *Shariah* requirements.

McDonald's in Singapore can be seen as a prime example; it has seen an influx of eight million patrons a year after obtaining a halal certification. Since being certified "halal, KFC, Burger King, and Taco Bell have all seen an increase of 20 percent in customers" (Hairalah, cited in Hazair, 2007a:13).

Consumers would turn their attention to a well-marketed product that does not have a halal mark, but they would read its ingredients, in contrast to purchasing one that has less credibility but sports a halal logo. It is therefore worthwhile that we take a look at each of the four tools of marketing mix that can be used to satisfy customers and company objectives.

Product, Packaging, and Quality

Success in marketing a halal product can be attributed to a strong brand name and, more importantly, knowing what the customers want.

When a Muslim consumer buys a halal product, he is doing so because of his commitment to Islamic principles and teachings, apart from his need for the product.

However, some halal food producers have developed a patronizing attitude toward the buyers, feeling that the consumers' lives will remain hard and dry since they will not be able to enjoy the product (El-Mouelhy 2007). Such an attitude needs to be changed. The quality must be there as well as the willingness of the suppliers to supply such quality halal products.

According to El-Mouelhy (2007), this patronizing attitude is very real and a common happening. It has affected the halal food trade between many countries. He cited that some of the oil-rich Muslim countries used to import poultry, meat, and dairy products from some of their fellow Muslim countries that were rich in agriculture and cattle.

The exporters had taken the importers' willingness to buy for granted and on occasions had failed to either maintain the quality or meet various other commitments. Despite numerous complaints, the exporters did little to improve or rectify the situation. Inadvertently, the buyers' trust is lost; and they started looking elsewhere, including to non-Muslim countries.

El-Mouelhy further argues that the failure of Muslim halal exporters to recognize that the consumer is in fact the final arbiter had led the switch to suppliers who believed in the ultimate rights of the consumer. Thus, non-Muslim suppliers who may not have heard or eaten halal food in their entire life have been very successful in supplying halal to the Muslim market. The reason: they knew the golden rule of marketing — that the consumer is king!

As a result, today in many Muslim countries, halal poultry, meat, dairy products, and other foods are predominantly imported from Europe, Australia, New Zealand, and America. And the consumers are happy because they are getting not only halal food but also high-quality food (El-Mouelhy 2007).

In terms of packaging, it is also considered tactless for producers to name their products after haram or forbidden foods, such as chicken ham, halal beef bacon, or alcohol-free beer. This can be misleading to the Muslim community as "halal consumers are quite sensitive to these issues" (Hairalah, cited in Hazair, 2007a:13).

The halal labels should not only be descriptive but also be clear and meaningful to the consumers. The technique is to clearly identify the source of the food elements, more so if the food components contain unfamiliar elements such as the E numbers, which "could cause confusion and problems for Muslim consumers" (Junaidah Hj Abu Bakar, cited in Han, 2007a:5).

Easily recognizable halal accreditation labels will promote the religious compliance for the Muslims; however, it needs to appear with a forward-looking font to differentiate it from other trademarks. Stylized Arabic fonts very much associated with Islam can be incorporated into the labels.

Promotion, Public Relations, and Advertising

Promotion and branding is the key to making products "click." "By creating a Halal brand, we (businesses) have the opportunity to touch lives of more people. Creating a trust mark for the Muslim community . . . it (Halal) could become its own power brand" (Bayman, cited in Hazair, 2007c).

Additionally, participating in expositions and seminars on halal products can only lead to more sales. It brings awareness to Muslims and non-Muslims alike of the availability of their halal products and the suppliers/wholesalers at both the national and international level.

Advertising is also key for marketing and sales. From the halal advertising perspective, strategy depends upon whether a particular market is Muslim-majority populated or it is a mix of different ethnicities or communities.

In a Muslim-majority case, where the total presence of non-Muslims is only marginal, it is appropriate to emphasize the halal nature and characteristics of the food so that it attracts the common folks in the society who forms the majority.

However, in a multi-religious society where Muslims are a significant proportion of the population, the product can be marked as halal on the label so that the members of the community are aware of its status as well as promote the product in the Muslim and ethnic media. Here, for the non-Muslims, the product's quality is to be emphasized.

Pricing

In terms of pricing, strong halal brands have to be created and be built upon. Brands can add value to a product, allowing the manufacturer to enjoy the ability to command a higher pricing for their products. Good halal branding, while commanding higher prices, can also attract or entice the non-Muslim consumers.

Place

As argued in Low (2007), companies selling halal products should capitalize on the Muslim Diasporas, that is, selling in Malay Muslim and/or Arab Muslim majority countries or Middle Eastern countries. In this way, the companies have an expanded market and a bigger playing field.

However, it should be noted that from the producers' point of view, there are two types of markets for halal food, i.e., markets in non-Muslim countries and markets in the Muslim countries (El-Mouelhy 2007).

In the case of the non-Muslim countries, the problem is serious because the Muslim communities are scattered. Thus, it is difficult to distribute through dealers because in many cases there are no dealers but only the scattered small retailers. The labor cost is also high that the price will become not competitive as compared to the same product that lacks halal attributes.

Despite these difficulties, one cannot disregard the huge potential it poses. The answer lies in making the product halal in the first place, as well as making it available for all (El-Mouelhy 2007). Marketers for halal product in non-Muslim countries should also participate in established exhibitions and conferences within their Muslim communities to build confidence and network.

For Muslim-dominated markets, business need to:

* avoid a patronizing attitude and be wary that the customer is king, honoring commitments on a regular basis,
* ensure and upkeep the product's quality, and
* know the culture of the local distributors. When dealing with these distributors, it is important to know their expectations and their way of saying yes and no. One should also be ready to learn how things can be made to move within any given culture.

Conclusion

Overall, businesses and marketers need to realize that halal marketing is very much like marketing for any other products, and the 4Ps of marketing mix should be applicable. They should also recognize that the Muslim consumers would be loyal when they always get the product they want, the supplier has kept his promise and supplied quality products, and the "halalness" of the product is unquestionable. There should be some form of halal certification and a respectable authority guaranteeing the producers' claims.

* *By Dr. Saad Al-Harran & Dr. Patrick Low, Faculty of Business, Economics and Policy Studies, Universiti Brunei Darussalam. The Halal Journal: January-February, 2008, Kuala Lumpur, Malaysia.*

6 HOW CAN WE TURN BRUNEI DARUSSALAM INTO A NATION OF NEW IDEAS?

PART 1

As a newcomer to Brunei Darussalam, I have observed that there are too many restaurants and catering services in practically every corner of the capital. Undoubtedly, restaurants provide us with delicious food to eat and enjoy while at the same time they enable us to have the energy to be active citizens in the community.

But to have too many restaurants competing with each other in a small market is something of a concern that requires serious attention from the policymakers—especially those who want to have a solid foundation for small and medium enterprises (SMEs) to grow and progress.

A few have succeeded to open not only one but two or three restaurants because they provide quality food and services, such as play areas for children so as to make dining enjoyable. Meanwhile, others struggle because of the tough competition.

The question is, how can we solve this problem of having too many restaurants and come up with new ideas that will enable small businesses to grow and be sustainable in a highly competitive marketplace? I am sure the government is keen to support new initiatives that will allow small businesses to grow and succeed locally while competing in the international market at the same time.

To every human being, Allah the Almighty has given the capacity to think and reflect. Allah says in the Quran:

Read: In the Name of your Lord who created. Created mankind from something blood clot which clings; Read! And your Lord is the Most Noble; who taught by the pen; taught mankind what he did not know. (Sura Al-Alaq 1-4)

The declaration or proclamation in the verse aforementioned was to be in the name of God the Creator; it was a call from God for the benefit of erring humanity. This declaration clearly indicates that God gave this commandment—through Prophet Muhammad (Pbuh)—to all mankind, regardless of faith, color, or ability to read and write.

Therefore, reading enables us to learn of Allah's gifts to mankind. Through reading, our limited knowledge will increase, and our viewpoint will widen. Through reading, we will see things that others can't see and reflect.

In a gist, reading is a gift and blessing from Allah that we need to utilize effectively every day. It is another endowment from God to us, just like the senses of hearing, looking, as well as the spirit and determination that drive us to serve Allah and our society. It is through reading that endless opportunities will be opened to us, more knowledge will be gained—giving us the additional strength and capacity to excel—and more ideas will transpire, making us stand out from the others.

It is also true that the more we read, the more we know while at the same time, the more we write, the further we go from those who don't read and write. So now we realized why Allah gave a clear command to Prophet Muhammad (Pbuh) to read—so as to gain knowledge.

The benefit of reading is infinite, but mainly it helps expand the mind and purify its thoughts, increases one's knowledge, and enhances both our memory and understanding. Through frequent reading, one develops the ability to acquire and process knowledge and to learn more about the different fields of knowledge and their application to life.

Why is Reading Important to Children?

Reading is vital for a child's mental development. It is a thinking activity that involves critical thinking (the decoding of words, word parts, phrases, and sentences) and creative thinking (the use of imagination, empathy, and problem solving). It is through reading that the child becomes involved in processing information, in investigating, in making connections, and in solving problems.

The discovery process the child passes through does not necessarily utilize the ideas he or she brings to the classroom; but it goes far beyond what he or she brought, contributed, and took away from the experience. Does the teacher know? Often no because of outdated teaching methods and practices, like learning by rote.

We need to show our children different ways of looking at the world, the many different ways of patterning their experience, and how to use — in a thoughtful way — different aspects of their intelligence.

Since Brunei Darussalam is blessed with natural resources, teachers need to take children outside the classroom to augment the knowledge they gained through reading by giving them a rich and varied experience with words and books. They need to share the meaning of the text by discussing what they learned.

Surely, learning via reading is not just a child-centered experience; it is a process of development, which lasts throughout life. Undoubtedly, fluent readers know not only more words and more about those words; they are able to reason from language. Such children progress far more quickly than those who rely on others for definitions of words.

On the contrary, poor readers are slow to apply thinking to reading and unwilling to make the cognitive effort needed to make sense of difficult texts.

Culture of Reading and Learning

While we are in the information age, parents, teachers, and caregivers have moral duties and responsibilities to empower children through reading and learning by spending valuable times with them at home, school, and public parks. Regrettably, children and teenagers today are spending hours on TV watching movies, playing computer games that teach them how to be violent to their peers, or moving around from one shopping mall to another wasting their valuable time.

These teenagers don't appreciate the importance of time and the priceless assets that Allah has given us, that is, reading and seeking knowledge.

We as parents and caregivers need to be role models and show them the real path of happiness through reading and implant the habit of reading and learning in their minds. We also need to create a conducive and healthy environment for the children and teenagers so they love and enjoy the journey of learning through reading by understanding the meaning of the texts.

We should encourage them to select the main ideas of the books in order to make a short summary. We need to keep the door open for the children to add their own thoughts and feelings, predicting what will come next, referring forward and backward, suggesting imagery and character responses. That requires modernization of public and school libraries so children love going to these learning centers where they can do their homework and research a topic of interest to them.

Prophet Muhammad (Pbuh) advises us to seek knowledge even if it requires us to travel to China in order to learn from their cultures and values. We need to give children cues on how to seek meaning from texts so their reading comprehension will be widened and they will appreciate that reading and seeking knowledge are powers in the world of today.

Can We Succeed to Do That?

For a small nation like Brunei, I believe the government has given all supports to its citizens to excel. It also welcomes any new initiatives through new ideas and innovation to see the nation progress in a global knowledge society. We also need to have mobile libraries accessible to children and teenagers in Bandar as well as the rural areas so children will benefit from going to the library and borrow books or stories in order to gain benefits and share their experiences with their peers.

Here we have a moral duty to make the journey to the libraries attractive by undertaking various programs such as storytelling, mathematical games, and reading competitions. During summer holidays, libraries need to develop programs for children to read books that interest them and give brief summary about it.

In doing so and through time and hard work and conducive environment, the nation will succeed in creating a thinking and knowledgeable society that can create wealth and share it in the community.

7 BRUNEI DARUSSALAM MAIN SOURCE OF NEW IDEAS

PART 2

Once we create a new culture of reading and seeking knowledge in the society, then the main sources of new ideas should not be a problem.

The starting point is high schools, colleges, vocational training institutions, and universities. This requires moving around these educational institutions, explaining to their principals and headmasters why new ideas are important to Brunei Darussalam and how we can achieve that.

We should start from the Science College, Sultan Saiful Rijal Technical College, Jerudong International School, and International School Brunei to name a few, to make students excited about the new program and what they have to do for their country in order to build Brunei as a nation of new ideas and business enterprise.

Surely, such motivations and incentives will undoubtedly make students happy to submit their ideas in the form of business proposals to the principals and headmasters.

A new group of experienced professionals from outside these institutions will be assigned the responsibility to examine these ideas, and if it is found financially viable, then it goes for further processing.

We should encourage students to work collectively in different fields such as science and technology and biochemistry with others in strategic marketing. They will learn the skills of working together for noble projects and assisting their government in building a knowledge-based society and sharing their thoughts and ideas together.

Here we need to promote the concept "cooperate locally in order to succeed internationally." I believe students can provide valuable assets that assist the nation to progress internationally at the global arena.

Investing in New Business Ideas

Small businesses in Brunei require intensive care and continued support from the government agencies such as the Ministry of Industry and Primary Resources and Brunei Economic Development Board (BEDB), which want to see this vital sector of the economy proactive in creating wealth to the nation even if it requires assistance from outside, that is, the tertiary sector.

The current practices of businesses such as food and beverages, and garment manufacturing in the marketplace are something of concern that requires attention by the policy makers as to where this sector is heading.

The only way out for the government agencies to explore is the student potentials through new business ideas scheme that we proposed and venture capital endeavors. These new innovative initiatives should be considered as alternatives or supplement sources of intellectual capital that the policy makers need to address in the coming years.

Undoubtedly, the students are the engine of economic development and the future business leaders, who are being confronted with various challenges and problems. They have to be given the opportunities and a conducive environment to excel because they are the main vehicle for change and hopes that the government should rely on to generate new intellectual wealth away from oil and gas industries.

The target groups are the schools mentioned above. These schools have been selected because of local and international outlook so they can work together.

Naturally, investment in human capital is a noble task that empowers students to excel. Often many have new ideas but have failed because of the lack of funds to start the business.

Therefore, there is an urgent need to set up Brunei Youth Venture Capital Company (BYVCC) that could provide the following services:

1. In-House Incubator: It provides students with access to superior resources, regular workshops focusing on start-up business, product development, market development teams, and intellectual property protection.

2. Access to new business partners who might be interested to finance the innovation that a student has developed. Such a new strategic alliance is vital to new partners. It is here where *musharakah* (partnership) Islamic contract will be signed between the student, who provides the intellectual capital through the new innovation that he or she comes up with, and the business partner, who provides the capital. Such a contract needs to be prepared by a lawyer who is specialized in intellectual property under the supervision of the principals and headmasters of the school that the student comes from. Student rights need to be protected as he or she will be business partner with the person who provides finance that could be government agencies or somebody from the corporate sector.

3. Opportunities for global media to write a story about the student innovation that comes from Brunei. No doubt, such motivation and incentives will encourage our students to innovate and put up new business proposals through working hard and understanding the concept of life that needs struggle in order to excel.

Finally, these gifted students need to be given a special status in the country and financial rewards for their hard work and their new innovation because the nation depends on them. They are the new breed of youth entrepreneurs who create wealth and share it responsibly in the community.

8 PROPOSED STRATEGIC ALLIANCE BETWEEN QATAR FOUNDATION FOR EDUCATION, SCIENCE, AND COMMUNITY DEVELOPMENT (QFESCD) AND ALJAZEERA INTERNATIONAL CHANNEL IS IMPORTANT FOR THE GOVERNMENT OF QATAR TO EXPLORE IN ORDER TO INVEST IN NEW INNOVATIVE IDEAS AND VENTURE CAPITAL TO FACE THE CHALLENGES OF THE TWENTY-FIRST CENTURY

We are living in the age of new ideas, venture capitals, young entrepreneurs, managing risks, and global media that promote those who create wealth and share it responsibly in the community to achieve just in the local and international market. These ingredients of success require new reading cultures that continue seeking knowledge and strategizing with other cultures to share information and experiences that is called in the modern language a knowledge-based society. Islamic finance needs to explore and promote in the age of Internet and wireless connections that link the citizens across the world whether in the east or the west, the north or the south, to enable them to connect together and learn from each other to achieve universal goals of finance with social responsibility.

Strategic alliances, business ventures, and innovative ideas are the lifeblood of the modern business world that needs to be well understood. It is not only politics and current affairs; among other interesting programs that Aljazeera

Arab Channel is good at that brought all Arabs together under one umbrella to speak their minds, but also financing these programs is vitally important as it is the heart of any business venture.

Therefore, Islamic finance with social responsibility (IFSR), technology, and innovation are the main components of the knowledge-based economy (that we are part and parcel of) that the government of Qatar needs to further develop as we have millions of people in the Muslim world who have new innovative ideas but lack finance to start their business ventures. It is here where the West has developed while the Muslim world was left behind among other things. At the same time, Islamic finance should work hand in hand with Non-Government Organizations (NGOs) and civil societies (who care for the environment and climate changes) to promote investment in social capital projects in other to reactivate the economies of the Muslim world that faces many challenges ahead.

All these efforts need an international discourse and intellectual dialogue; and the best platform is Aljazeera International Channel (ALJIC), which is governed by the satellite televisions and the Internet that have connected the Islamic community of 1.5 billion people across the globe with the rest of other human beings to discuss issues of global concerns — that is, finance (as a human right), business with social responsibility, farming, food security, and environmental crisis in the Muslim world.

Indeed, the language of the new era is collaboration, cooperation, strategic marketing and thinking, and active participation in any business ventures that needs to be cemented to enable small nations as well as those individuals with new innovative ideas to grow and contribute toward the development of their economies.

The paper, firstly, highlights the importance of strategic alliance; secondly, we discuss the global outlook as to how Qatar can position itself in the world map as a knowledge-based nation and a land of innovative ideas. Thirdly, we analyze the new role of IFSR and why investment in social capital is vitally important in the challenging world. We have selected four Muslim countries that Qatar needs to consider for human capital investment purposes — that is, Egypt (the brain and heart of the Arab world), Syria, Turkey, and Malaysia; and we will explain why these countries have been selected. Fourthly, we will discuss the new role of ALJIC as a global media player and a new promoter of successful entrepreneurs and venture capitalists in the Muslim world to show others what the real Islamic finance is. Finally, the challenges ahead and conclusions and policy recommendations will be suggested.

1.   Introduction

"Strategic alliance" (SA) can be defined as a forged powerful relationship with business entities based on mutual trust, long-term vision, strategic relationships, world-class and sustainable competitive advantages for all the partners, relationships which have a further separate and positive impact outside the partnership or alliance. In the context of social responsibility, global media can provide private companies or young entrepreneurs with new innovative business ideas the ability to create a strong advertising and marketing campaign to succeed at the local and international market.

2.   Global Outlook

With the Qatar leadership of the Emir Sheik Hamad bin Khalifa Al-Thani, he realized that the real wealth is not oil and gas, but rather it is the human and intellectual capital that needs to be promoted. Qatar has started this long-term journey through the establishment of Aljazeera Arabic Channel (ALJAC) in Dhoa (capital of Qatar) in 1996 by bringing the brain of Arab intellectuals who are well-experienced journalists and used to work in BBC Arabic Channel service in London to that country. Qatar today is considered to be a role model in the Arab world not only in global media through ALJAC but also in the political arena that made that country well respected as new regional power in the Arab world. It is the ALJAC that breaks through the barriers of monopoly that is controlled by the multinational corporations (MNC) that represent the interest of MNC and not the general public.

Surely under the Emir's leadership, he realized that the global media represented by CNN and BBC is not our media but theirs. It is also true that the mission of the emir of Qatar and his wife Her Highness Sheikha Mozah Bint Nasser Al-Missned went far beyond ALJAC when they decided to establish the Qatar Foundation for Education, Science, and Community Development (QFESCD) in 1995 to provide educational opportunities and improve the quality of life for the people of Qatar and other Arabs in the region.

Therefore, the agenda, the vision, and the long-term mission of the emir of Qatar are clear — that is, to make QFESCD the engine of economic growth with a strategic aim: making **the country as a land of new innovative ideas.** The main reason is obvious, that is, to prepare the people of Qatar and the region to meet the challenges of an ever-changing world and accept new ideas in order to make Qatar a leader in innovative education and research.

From the above analyses, the Qatar leadership has also realized that in the global knowledge economy, which we are part and parcel of, the ingredients of success shown under must work together to create wealth and share it responsibly in the community and far beyond into the globe as illustrated in diagram one.

Global Knowledge Economy

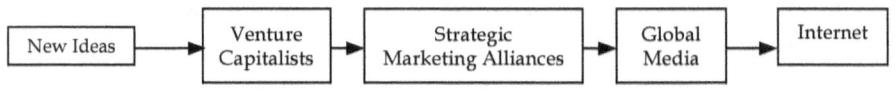

Diagram One

The new area of IFSR and investment in new business ideas has no limit in the global village environment that can start from Canterprise at Canterbury University in New Zealand (*www.canterprise.ac.nz*) where the business ideas are commercialized to Telford Rural Polytechnic in New Zealand (*www.telford. ac.nz*) of hands-on experience that youths are looking for from the new long-term vision of social capital. To untapped human resources through *Sanduq* (box fund), a microfinance innovation in Jabal Al-Hoss, Syria, which needs to be funded as a community development project in order to give opportunities to underprivileged people in Aminah and Riad to obtain credit to further develop their business venture to assist them to have stable financial income that brings rural families together, sharing common goals and aspiration (Imady, O. and Hans Dieter Seible).

Undoubtedly, these proposed new strategic alliances allow us to learn from others of different cultures as life is a learning process. We want to learn why they have succeeded and what is the pathway to achieve that, has started from Silicon Valley in California, USA and far beyond that is Islamic finance has to do with social-responsibility. We want to see more venture capitalists and youth entrepreneurs working together creating wealth and sharing it responsibly in the Muslim world. We are also keen to bring a new breed of youth to Islamic finance through the proper utilization of the human assets who can manage their business ventures effectively and understand the concept of life is struggle until death through hard work and long-term practical vision (Al-Harran, S.).

To assist us in our innovative and creative new business ventures by working together with others and the final aim is making Qatar as a new global Islamic financial hub is indeed timely and rewarding task, but how we can achieve that is what diagram two explain. We proposed a new role for QFESCD:

Qatar as New Global Islamic Financial Hub

```
┌─────────┐    ┌──────────────────┐    ┌────────────────┐    ┌────────────────┐
│ QFESCD  │───▶│ (Consultancy and │───▶│ Internal Panel │───▶│ Independent    │
│         │    │ Supervisory Roles)│    │                │    │ Technology     │
└─────────┘    └──────────────────┘    └────────────────┘    └────────────────┘

┌────────────────┐    ┌──────────────────────┐    ┌────────────────────┐
│ Experts (Review│───▶│ Qatar International   │───▶│ Arab Investors or  │
│ Panel)         │    │ Islamic Bank         │    │ Industry partners  │
└────────────────┘    └──────────────────────┘    └────────────────────┘

┌──────────────────────┐    ┌────────────────┐    ┌────────────────┐
│ Celebrating Success  │    │ New breed of   │    │ Wealth Creation│
│ through the new role │───▶│ Entrepreneurs  │───▶│ & Social       │
│ of International      │    │                │    │ Responsibility │
│ Al-Jazeera Channel    │    └────────────────┘    └────────────────┘
└──────────────────────┘
```

Diagram Two

The QFESCD newly proposed model will be consultancy as well as supervisory roles that look after the project processing to ensure an efficient system of monitoring and follow-up put in place. It receives the new innovative business ideas (from different parts of the Muslim world or Muslim minorities who live in the West) application forms and processes it. They need to hire gifted Muslim and non-Muslim consultants who mostly are living in the West who have successful records as entrepreneurs in their business ventures, practitioners, and Technologists and venture capitalists who are well experience in global business trends so they can give proper professional advice on these projects based on economic and financial soundness. They have to be stakeholders in the new business ventures to set up in order to ensure its success and to share the profits and losses if any that put them in a challenging position. They have to work hard for the betterment of the Muslim world that is based on a fair and just financial system.

Once the independent technologists and review panel experts clear these projects that they are financially and economically viable and are ready for financing, it is here where the Qatar International Islamic Bank and Arab investors (or industry partners) come to the picture by financing these projects. After the project is financed, post monitoring and follow-up must follow to ensure proper implementation and disbursement of fund. Here again QFESCD needs to hire experienced Muslim professionals who specialize in operational matters especially monitoring and follow-up to keep track records for the project's performances and check and balance on a quarterly basis to ensure it generates profit to the stakeholders that include all parties involved.

It is here where QFESCD can give chance for talented Muslims to submit their business proposals for assessment. Once they have been found viable, then a youth can see big hope because he or she is no longer unemployed but as employable person who is an active partner in his or her business ventures. It is here where the new role of global media represented by ALJIC comes in, that is, to promote them because they achieve success not only for themselves but also for the economies where they come from.

This kind of model keeps everybody busy because he or she is a stakeholder in the business ventures they want to succeed in making **Qatar as an innovative nation, centre of excellence and a role model for the Muslim world.** These Muslim thinkers must be independent without any political interference because they want to create wealth and share it responsibly far beyond into the Muslim world. They get shares and the more they do well in any business venture, the more they get shares. These kinds of rewards will make them work hard and appreciate their new role as wealth creator to mankind who is under stress whether in Asia, Africa and Middle east due to economic and financial injustices prevailing in the current world. They want to apply the profit-sharing system based on Islamic principles of sharing and caring for others.

3. The New Role of Islamic Finance with Social Responsibility (IFSR)

From the above assessment, it is clear that what we are proposing is a new agenda for Islamic finance, that is, IFSR by investing in the human capital (not in a mega-high-rise building) in the Muslim world whether in Egypt which is considered to be the heart and the brain of the Arab world in science, arts, and applied technology. Indeed, investments in agricultural development and textile industry are vital in order to see the Egyptian economy reactivate in providing food sufficiency to its citizens that can feed its growing population. The second example is Turkey, which is considered to be another role model in the Muslim world that needs investment in its economy to grow in order to compete in the European market, and therefore investments in rural farming and agribusinesses are indeed timely for the country. Syria has taken huge responsibility for the Arab causes and paid high costs that its economy needs urgent financial support so that it will grow to support its citizens and others. Therefore, investments in food technology and agriculture and skilled manpower are vital in order to support the government policies by welcoming Arab investments in different sectors of the economy in order to generate employment to their growing citizens. Last but not least, Malaysia has made headway in electronic industries and now is at a crossroad, facing many challenges whether economically, financially, or socially. It also needs financial support to enable her to become a role model in technological innovation, agricultural development, and halal food processing that needs investment in human capital and creativity in order to see its economy growing at a fast record and moving into the right direction. Malaysia today needs future business leaders who are productive in innovative ideas so that the dream of building a thinking nation will be realized.

All these human capital investments whether in Egypt, Turkey, Syria, or Malaysia can lead **Qatar to be the valley and center for innovation and business ventures for the whole Muslim world,** what is explained in diagram three.

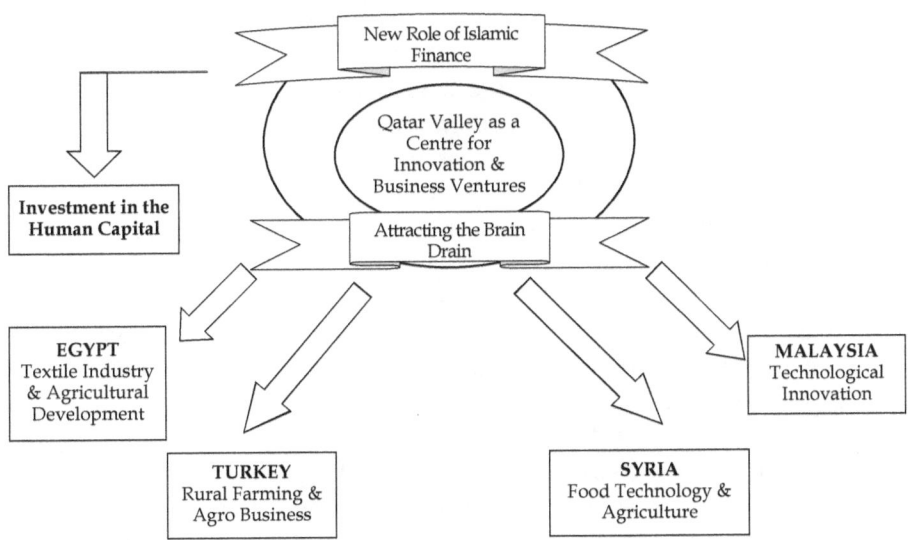

Diagram Three

4.   Aljazeera International Channel in the World Map

Today's world is all about innovations, creative ideas, and strategic alliances that can be translated to business ventures and promotions in the global media. Oil-rich countries have huge financial assets, which are estimated at US$97.3 billion by the end 2007 according to Moody's Investors Service (*The Brunei Times*), and the market grew 15 percent over the past three years, but no tangible results have been achieved so far. We share the opinion that Islamic finance has a moral duty and social responsibility to channel some of these funds for productive investments at a grassroots level to bring changes in the global setting as wealth is power that needs to be spread to wider communities to empower people so they can see Islam as a functional faith as well as a way of life and to ensure it is well managed by competent and professional people to ensure its success. That requires setting up an Islamic consultancy house (ICH) as an independent arm of QFESCD.

Indeed, investments in technological innovations whether in agricultural industry, agribusiness, or food processing are vitally important as the Muslim world is facing endless problems that start from food crisis, water shortage, and environmental changes that adversely affect the underprivileged people and shatter their lives. Such timely investment in social capital programs through Islamic microfinance enterprises is essential in order to create millions of jobs for Muslim youths who are unemployable, looking now for business ventures.

On the other hand, other youths who have new business ideas but lack finances that IFSR needs to support them financially to enable them to become active partners in the business ventures in order to succeed. In doing so, the global citizens can see Islamic finance start to have a social agenda and impact far beyond by serving a wider community, not in spending in mega-high-rise buildings that empower the rich to be richer at the expense of the poor.

It is here where the new role of ALJIC should be; it is to promote those entrepreneurs in the rural-farming areas of Asia, Africa, and the Middle East who are unprivileged to succeed and bring them in the front line, telling the world about their success stories and the hard work they have put in. We need to show others what success means in Islam and what sharing of wealth leads to by developing a new Web site for the new innovators, venture capitalists, and successful Muslim entrepreneurs. ALJIC has a moral duty to tell the citizens of the world about their success stories in the Muslim world, about small and medium enterprises (SMEs) business ventures or women in handicraft businesses who want to sell their products through the Internet and going out of poverty trap (Al-Harran, S., Alfred Yong Foh Sen & Seri Anne Masri).

In doing so, the global citizens can see through ALJIC the difference between their media and ours. It is the social agenda that mixed finance with social capital and promotes investment in community development in order to achieve fairness and justice in the global arena not only in finance but also in other social programs.

Therefore, the new role of Aljazeera is vitally important for Qatari leadership in the challenging world by inviting innovators, venture capitalists, industrialists, and those with new ideas whether they are from the East or the West, Arabs or non-Arabs, Muslims or non-Muslims, and put them in a on a weekly basis to discuss about environment crisis, solar and wind energy, and Islamic microfinance enterprises as shown in diagram four.

Aljazeera's New Innovation Program (Think Tank)

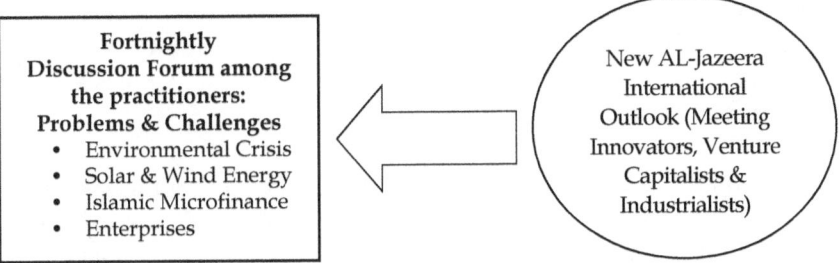

Diagram Four

Riz Khan's program on Aljazeera International Channel is the starting point. But it requires a different format and presentation that need further refinement by bringing intellectual Muslim practitioners and venture capitalists that mostly are living in the West to Qatar to handle such an important program that requires one and a half hour every weekend. We are keen to see changes in the direction of the whole program; and the main emphasis is innovation, creativity, and venture capital financing (in the Muslim world).

Today the Muslim world is facing endless challenges from youth unemployment to poverty and hunger and starvation without any solution in the horizon apart from endless meetings and conferences and worships that achieve very limit. Such timely debate and intellectual discourse is vital, but the whole discussion should not only talking only but a **plan of action through Islamic project financing**. It is here where Islamic microfinance enterprises (IMFEs) come to be to support new business initiative to ensure its success. We have to adopt a new strategy, that is, small is beautiful.

Many professional Muslim thinkers today start to question the concept of "economic development" that comes from the West imposed on us for the last five decades because we are powerless even though Allah Almighty has given us endless natural resources to effectively utilize. We also know well it is their models of economic development, not ours, that have led us from one disaster to another, costing us billions of dollars that are totally wasted, not to forget about the human suffering because we are sadly followers, not leaders that Allah Almighty wants us to be.

While others are seriously concerned as to which direction we are heading in this world of injustice, where the gap between the haves and the have-nots is widening, are we living safe in our homes, or do we need to have security guards to provide us security? Some affluent people think that as long as our families and children are fine, why should we care for others? But what kind of self-centered is. If we want our lives protected by security guards while there are millions of people are dying in pain and suffering that each of us seen on daily basis in that we are seeing in TV channels every day.

Regrettably, the consequences of following their economic development models have damaged our environment that has been made millions of people live misery today. A good example is Indonesia and what this Muslim country is experiencing in terms of landslide and earthquake is the outcome of proper planning to destabilize the whole country that has already started in 1960. Who has done that and what is the motive behind it is of no interest to us. Now we realized that their path of profit maximization is the path of destruction that has made mankind pay high cost and endless suffering. What we want to promote is profit-sharing system with social responsibility to look after the environment and come up with alternative source of energy like solar and wind to save the plants and ease endless suffering in Africa, Asia, and Middle East.

For how long we will continue to be a powerless nation (while seeing others are economies are in recession now due to poor financial and economic management) though we have huge financial assets searching for conducive environment and productive investment. The world today is all about financing first and politics second — not what is currently prevailing in most of the Muslim world. We want to see Islamic finance for the development of the human capital in order to reduce poverty and youth unemployment in the Muslim world that has reached unacceptable levels without any tangible results on the horizon due to lack of long-term vision and the failure of economic policies. Undoubtedly, environment crisis and climate changes, solar and wind energy, and Islamic microfinance enterprises are hot topics that need to be promoted in investment in research and development to save the humanity from the challenging future.

5. The Challenges Ahead

Youth unemployment is one of the most important challenges that face Muslim governments whether it is rich (in natural resources) or poor (in utilization of its human capital) without any tangible solutions in the horizon. The youth must work and find jobs that have to come from the private initiative funded by Islamic banks or community banks that need to look after the interest of the people. The government has a moral duty to create conducive climate for the business to succeed as work is an honor and dignity to mankind. In Islam, work is considered part of worship to Allah Almighty. Those who work hard get more reward (from Allah in this life and in the hereafter) than those who worship him. Allah (the creator, sustainer, and provider) knows best what is good for us. He encourages mankind to strive hard in life in order to provide sustenance and income to our families and children (Al-Harran, S.).

There are many reasons as to why youth unemployment has reached such unacceptable level among other things; it is the failure of our educational curricula system in the Muslim world that has not allowed students to think critically and creatively through the rote-learning system that made students only interesting in memorizing the text without fully understanding its meaning.

On the contrary, the learning process in the West is done through thinking skills and reflecting that students are passing through which allow them the use of library facilities heavily to do their own homework. Therefore, Qatar as a role model to the Muslim world has a moral duty and social responsibility to set up thinking schools, hands-on experience and finance it. The concept should be similar to Telford Rural Polytechnic, New Zealand model, she also need to help financially applied science, and technology institutions in Egypt, Syria, Turkey, and Malaysia in order to see an inflow of new ideas coming in from Muslim intellectual to the nerve centre of innovation in Doha as shown in diagram five.

Intellectual Capital

Diagram Five

This new culture needs to be adopted in our schools as well as creating a conducive environment that encourage students to think creatively, and in the process, those who have innovative ideas can be classified and taken to different classrooms. They are called gifted students. They need new refinement of their skills, and the schools should provide them with tools and instruments of success. New Zealand has done a wonderful work to promote gifted students, and these are few Web sites for learning purposes: *www.giftedchildren.org.nz* and *www. tki.org.nz/r/gifted/handbook* and gifted talented students: meeting their needs in New Zealand schools *www.learningmedia.co.nz*. These students are the wealth creators of the society and nations that the country is look after them, as shown in diagram six.

Innovation is the language of the information age

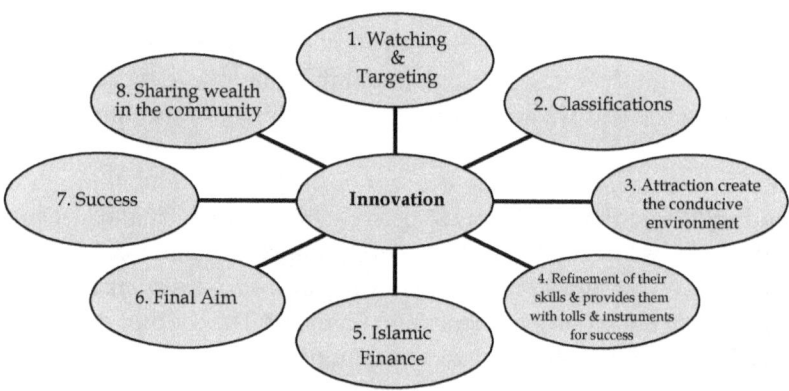

Diagram Six

It is here where Islamic finance should start, that is, investment in social capital at the intermediate and high school and vocational training where innovation can be easily discovered.

Sadly some of our educationists have always put down a student who has new innovative ideas because it might threaten him or her teacher or the whole school management, and therefore they have created a culture of fear and worry in the classroom environment where students feel bored in the room because there is nothing for them, and that needs to be changed to "a classroom without walls" that allows students to be creative. This problem is not only at our intermediate or high schools but also at universities and polytechnics. Some of the professors create a culture of background thinking, and the outcome is obvious, that is, the youth brain stops thinking and the mind becomes unproductive. The story goes further. The banking system has not been set up to support innovators rather that the addressing middle-class citizens' needs and the rich, and this is why these institutions were set up in urban areas and in big cities — to serve the middle class and the rich to be richer (Al-Harran, S.).

What the author is suggesting is that learning from other cultures is vitally important especially in the area of vocational training which the Muslim world needs most. It is called hands-on experience to enable students to learn the applied skill of education. At the same time IFSR needs to support any initiative financially, and the outcome will be a new breed of successful entrepreneurs who are well equipped to manage business ventures successfully. It is here where QFESCD needs to explore by collaborating with Qatar International Islamic Bank to finance vocational training institutions such as Telford Rural Polytechnic (*www.telford.ac.nz*), with Islamic finance inputs to create a new breed of young entrepreneurs who manage risks successfully. Indeed, certificate courses in agriculture farming where students obtain skills such as livestock handling, shearing, welding, fencing, pasture management, animal reproduction, and weed and pest management, just to name a few, are vitally important as we are facing crisis in food security.

We believe vocational training institutions and polytechnics are the answer to skilled manpower crisis in the Muslim world, and New Zealand can assist in providing tailor-made twinning program with Christchurch Polytechnic Institute of Technology (*www.cpit.ac.nz*) to alleviate youth unemployment. Applied courses such as certificate in pretrade plumbing, gas fitting, and drain laying; fitness instructing; and building trading are of great demands in the global market.

Conclusions and Recommendations

The paper is practical and has policy implications. It has been written based on the author's long experience in the field of Islamic finance and work with youth entrepreneurs. The suggestions made need to be critically examined by the policy makers in the government of Qatar; Qatar Foundation for Education, Science, and Community Development; and the Aljazeera top management and practitioners and successful business leaders in order to form a **strategic committee** to assess the overall proposed paper in order to come up with a **plan of action**.

The Muslim world is in a stage of crisis financially, economically, and socially. Each day 820 million people in the developing world who mostly are in the Muslim countries do not have enough food to eat. Indeed, oil-price rocketing, a perfect of food scarcity, global warming, and world population explosion are plunging humanity into the biggest crisis in human history by pushing up food prices and spreading hunger and poverty from rural areas into cities (*The Sunday Herald* [Scotland]). The world is not a safe place anymore; adding to that are the imposed wars of the Muslim world from different directions. The Qatar leadership of Emir Sheik Hamad bin Khalifa Al-Thani has to play a major role in the global setting as what the author has proposed in this interesting model will take Qatar to a different path and become a role model for the whole world.

We are ready to give a presentation or public talk to the policy makers in the government of Qatar, QFESCD, and Aljazeera in order to see these applied models implemented, and the Muslim world economies will reactivate to give hopes to millions of youths who are looking for business opportunities. At the same time, IFSR has a moral duty to act now in such a critical moment of our history. If such timely decision will be made by the Qatar leadership, then the citizens of the world can see that Islamic finance with social responsibility has a global agenda; that's what Islam as a way of life is all about.

9 MUSLIM YOUTH: CHALLENGES AND SOLUTIONS

Youths are the engine of economic development. They are the future leaders of the Muslim world, which is being confronted with various challenges and problems. Many have lost faith in their governments and are looking elsewhere for dynamic changes in their socioeconomic setting. Poverty, a man-made problem, is on the rise without any serious efforts being made to resolve the predicament. The number of hungry people remains high in a world where food is in surplus.

Unemployment among the youths is a dilemma for policy makers. Even affluent societies are worried about the direction in which the youths are heading. Are they utilizing their time effectively, or are they wasting it? The planet is at stake due to the destruction of the environment, conflicts, and misunderstanding of the concept of "development" in Islam. The deterioration of living conditions is apparent and is accompanied by an explosion of corruption and threat to public money, a trust from Allah Almighty as wealth, to be managed and distributed by trustworthy parties to all people.

Youth in Islam

The above-mentioned unhealthy conditions, on both the economic and social levels, give rise to one main question – in which direction are the Muslim communities moving in? The time has come for us to urgently address the problem and change the lives of thousands of people. A plausible option is to maintain Islam as way of life.

The first effort should be to equip Muslim youths with applied skills to enable them to be problem solvers and successful marketers. Islam considers development of resources as a key factor for economic and social prosperity. Prophet Muhammad (Pbuh) achieved this with his companions. Khalifah Omar

Bin Khatab, as a result of his strong personality, trustworthiness, and long-term mission, succeeded in creating many leaders after him. His model of "leader among the leaders" is a powerful managerial concept.

This model needs to be examined by contemporary business and management schools to learn and understand how these leaders achieved success. Islam should be diffused throughout the world, and the Muslim youths should be a role model. It is through dialogue, tolerance, trust, and cooperation that the message of Islam can be spread.

The main factors behind the success of these Muslim leaders were their vision and long-term mission to accomplish their objectives. Faith was no doubt the driving force of their accomplishment — belief in Oneness of Allah (*Tawhid*), belief in the hereafter, hard work, and discipline all contributed to their achievement. In return, Allah empowered them and gave them the strength and sense of direction to succeed.

In the Quran, Allah clearly says:

> They were youths, who believed in their Lord, and we advanced them
> in guidance. We gave them strength in their hearts. (Sura 18:13-14)

The Qur'an clearly puts that the Creator of the universe provides for whom he wills and carries them higher and higher on the road to Truth. Faith is cumulative. Each step leads to a higher rank, by the grace and mercy of Allah.

These past Muslim leaders were not afraid to speak out openly and protest the truth, which they clearly practiced in their daily lives. Thus, there was a close relationship between faith and mission in their lives. Their basis in life was to worship Allah (*Ibadaat*) and deal with people (*Muamallat*). The balance approach that they upheld liberated them from oppression and gave them the needed independence to be strong politically and financially.

Allah also says in the Quran that:

> Truly the best of men are tie who are strong and trustworthy.
> (Sura Qasas 26)

In the Qur'an, Allah relates the story of Prophet Shuaib, describing how he trusted Prophet Moses as his employee and how both parties had mutual confidence in each other. Strong and trustworthy, Moses had proved himself to be both a reliable employee and human being. This story should be heeded by each youth in order to be strong in faith and belief in Allah. Islam promotes fairness and uprightness when dealing with mankind regardless of race, religion, color, and creed; and this message should be propagated among the present youth to make this world a better place to live in.

Modern Youth

Technology is fast taking place, and the youths are the main target of this development. A large number of modern youths are out of control, living in a spiritual vacuum and under poor conditions. Many parents are struggling hard from one job to another to support their families. There are currently many professionals who are worried about the future while others are threatened by the role technology is playing as they are distressed that technology might one day take over their jobs. The Westerners, however, generally do not see such a phenomenon as threat; rather, it is an opportunity to lead their lives more freely.

Youths today have better access to computers and are therefore open to immoral and violent materials, which can affect their behavior both at home and school. As such, parents and teachers sometimes have little control over the children's behavior and discipline. The culture of violence and bullying has become a norm in most schools in the West, and no solution has been found to curb this phenomenon.

Modern media, controlled by few, has played its role in destroying the moral fabric of youth in the society. Communication between parents and children has collapsed, and breakdown in family units is prevalent in the society.

Sadly in New Zealand there are a high percentage of teenagers involved in drugs. In the USA too, more and more children are involved in such activities, unaware of the risks involved. The moral ethics of the youth are at stake, having lost the direction.

It is unfortunate that these social diseases have found a place among the Muslim communities throughout the world. As a result of globalization and modern technology, Muslim youths are being faced with foreign influence and values that have adverse effect to the Islamic faith. Leaders and policy makers are in a quandary as to how these problems could be overcome.

Islamic Views

Despite the negative impact of technology, no doubt it does have some benefits. Through technology, within seconds, we are able to communicate with people from different parts of the world. We also get to share and spread knowledge and information to the rest of world. Technological development in various fields such as medicine has certainly changed and saved the lives of many people on earth. All these benefits are of course something that are welcomed but at a cost.

Together with the benefits that it brings, technology also has some adverse effects that are entirely targeting the youth. The moral decadence and loss of family and cultural values are already taking place in the West and are spreading slowly to the Muslim societies. Acknowledging the urgency to overcome the problems facing the Muslim youth, Muslim parents, leaders, and scholars should now take it upon them to listen to the youth and attempt to resolve the misfortune that we are being faced with.

Islamic Finance: Proposal to Establish Center for Youth Entrepreneurs

Our youths are a gift from our Creator to us. We are responsible and accountable to Allah in molding the young. This is a responsibility of all adults. We need them for the future — we need them to be successful leaders, entrepreneurs, educators, and, above all, good humans, who will assume responsibility to make the world a better place for the generations to come.

Although there are a large number of venture capitalists, business leaders, and marketers in this world, they lack the skills, ethics, and discipline to shoulder their tasks. An answer to this is Islamic finance. Islamic finance seems the best alternative to solve this problem as the Islamic financial system is based on the Shariah principles, the principles of the Creator, which are fair, ethical, rational, and accurate.

Islamic finance will give the Muslim youth the needed boost to function and manage their resources in accordance to their faith. This equitable financial system would certainly bring about changes and supersede the present capitalist economic system.

The Importance of Marketing Research

For any system to succeed, a strong leadership is incumbent. Faith — or belief in Allah — should be the foundation. Business skills have to be identified;

the requirements and framework to suit the needs of the youth must be established.

In establishing an Islamic financial system for instance, the leader should clearly define a point of reference so that the youth will understand the concepts being carried out and incorporate their tasks constructively.

Motivation is another element that is required in encouraging the youth to be earnest in their efforts. The youth should also be taught to be receptive to different opinions and to be open to changes.

For any system to thrive, monitoring and evaluation is vital to keep track of its progress. In advocating the Islamic financial system, it is likely that the youth will develop and sustain their moral and ethical responsibilities toward empowering the society that they live in, thus indirectly establishing a just system for the entire world.

10 SUCCESSFUL WAYS TO ENTREPRENEURSHIP

We are living in the information age, where knowledge is vital. Every day we hear of new software being developed, new products being introduced into the market, and new innovation announced. With these developments, we tend to raise one important question—why do some people succeed in certain areas while others do not? Is it their mind-set, or is it the environment that they are in? Generally, the key reasons for their success are opportunity, initiative, and conducive setting for a new venture.

In the conventional system, investment is crucial for the social and economic development of a country. Entrepreneurs play a substantial role in the circulation and maintenance of the country's resources. Islam, being a religion of wisdom and research, advocates its followers to strive for knowledge and accomplish a good livelihood.

In the Qur'an, God tells us to continuously seek knowledge and strive in life so that we serve our purpose of living in this world and prepare ourselves for the eternal life in the hereafter. It is through knowledge that we become aware of our Creator and the universe. Truly, it is Allah, the Creator and Provider, who has endowed men with the intellect or the faculty to think so that we become rational beings. But above all, Allah has endowed human beings with "spirit" or "soul," without which our purpose and actions in life would be futile. In short, the essence of Islam is to base all our actions in accordance to the teachings of Allah and to focus our aims toward the worshipping of our Creator in living a righteous life.

Although investment is a new concept in Islam, it has been in operations for the last three decades. The concept can be traced back to the time of our Prophet. He was a successful entrepreneur not because of his wealth but due to his integrity, capability, and cooperative behavior. These characteristics made him a well-known entrepreneur among his community. As a man of faith and principle, Prophet Muhammad (Pbuh) was noble both as a human and trader.

Venture capital is also a new phenomenon in Islam. Although Islamic banks are trying their best to increase their market shares and service their customers in a more efficient manner but the sad reality is limited fund were invested in this mode of financing. Venture capital firms seem to be providing financing to other firms but for very low returns.

Banks were established to provide credit to both urban and rural communities in order to improve their socioeconomic status. Growth in the banking sector, however, has been slow. Although Islamic banking is different from the conventional system in terms of its mission and objectives, the concept has not been made known. Islamic banking, for the last three decades, has been promoted only among urban citizens. A large portion of the rural community is still vague about this concept and is unaware of the alternatives available to them.

In line with the laws of the Creator, the *Shariah,* Islamic banks should operate using these principles as their base or foundation:

a. **Leadership**
   Islamic banks should lead the corporate sector in terms of commitment and responsibility to safeguard humanity from exploitation, corruption, and injustice. The banks should act as leaders in maintaining justice and fair play in the society.

b. **Market Oriented**
   The operational staff of Islamic banks should be part of the society and not alienated from the community. They should be market oriented and should strive for productivity.

c. **Partnership**
   Partnership is necessary in any business or trade. Men need to be partners in business to be motivated to play their role as a vicegerent of Allah in bringing about goodness and justice to the people of the world.

Islamic Financial System and a New Class of Entrepreneurs

In a society where knowledge is a priority, a just economic system is substantial. A large number of Muslims are ambitious and innovative and wish to start their own businesses and become successful entrepreneurs. They, however, lack motivation and encouragement to achieve their objectives.

In establishing a successful Islamic financial system, Muslim entrepreneurs and business leaders have a moral responsibility to uphold uprightness and virtue in the society they live in. In ensuring that the system is balanced and free from corruption, the society too has a responsibility to educate and inform the young of the essence of business and trade in Islam.

Once the youth are taught and trained in line with the principles of Islam, there will emerge a new class of Muslim entrepreneurs in the society. These entrepreneurs will be not only strong in faith but also competent and productive. As Islam is a religion of transaction *(Muamalat)*, these young new entrepreneurs would act honorably and manage their business fairly with a strong team spirit.

Islam is a way of life, and Muslims should be role models to others regardless of faith, race, and color. In order for Islamic financial system to prevail, Muslim entrepreneurs should be examples and act in an admirable manner so that others would follow suit.

11   CAN WE SUCCEED TO MAKE QATAR A ROLE MODEL TO THE MUSLIM WORLD?

The Muslim world (MW) today is in a stage of disarray financially, politically, and socially. It is looking for a leader that has long-term goals to help ease the human suffering that has reached to unacceptable level to the rest of the Muslim countries. Who has achieved economic prosperity and wealth creation to his own citizens first? Second, who can provide other nations some sign of hopes and aspiration through providing financial assistance to them by circulating the wealth that Allah Almighty has given to him or his own country in order to achieve social justice. Regrettably, the MW is weak and powerless and has little to say in its local financial and political affairs or nothing to the rest of the world as long as they can't feed their own people, and they have lost contact with the masses, and often internal decisions are taken outside their boundaries.

The current food crisis that has suddenly hit the MW economies by surprise has shown without any doubt how weak they are. Some have admitted and are puzzled what to do next because of the public hunger and civil unrest that are looming. Others have a great faith in international agencies that can find solution to their internal problems through conferences or economic forums without realizing that these agencies have little to offer apart from talking only with no action.

What we have seen in the international arena surprises me and make me wonder simply because one agency blames the other while the poor and the needy suffer most in Africa, Asia, and Middle East. Some of those in power argue why we have left agriculture investment all these years while others believe that an international conference on the issue of food crisis will resolve the economic deadlock, and that illusion will lead to further complication due to the public frustration.

The financial scenario of the MW is not different from other sectors of the economy where research and development (R&D) and science and technology are in the crisis stage with limited financial resources to do research and development. Sadly these economies are in the stage of collapse also and ready for further humiliation, submission, poverty, and hunger. That has already started in many economies without any hopes on the horizon except a few cases of success that might be highlighted in the final chapter of this book (11).

Ironically, the powerful nations are looking for this unique moment that the MW is in. For them this is a great opportunity to effectively utilize the natural resources of Middle East, Asia, or Africa. Muslims today have underestimated the importance of market (*Suok*), and even our current education system has failed to appreciate the importance of market forces, and this is why we have youth unemployment among other things.

Regrettably, youth unemployment has reached a level that has made HH Sheikha Mozah Bint Nasser al-Missned (the wife of the emir of Qatar Sheikh Hamad bin Khalifa Al-Thani and the chairperson of Qatar Foundation for Education, Science, and Community Development) to highlight these new demanding challenges that face Qatar today during the opening session of the two-day event co-hosted by Silatech and the *Financial Times* at the Ritz-Carlton in Qatar on Monday, 2 June 2008. Her Highness pointed out, "This region is currently experiencing a staggering rate of 25% unemployment among youth" (Nour Abuzant, *www.gulf-time*). Such statement is clear indication that the matter seriously needs to be addressed by perhaps a think tank forum by her and the government of Qatar. Furthermore, in one of other states in that region, the youth unemployment has already reached 35 percent without any solution on the horizon.

Therefore, the powerful nation is in a new era of colonization; and control of MW natural resources has already started by imposed wars in Iraq, Afghanistan, and now Darfur region in Sudan. These wars are purely because of financial motives and nothing else — that is, full control of oil field and other natural resources that the powerful nations want from us. For them, we are a huge market potential; it is now time to implement that policy that they have set up for six decades.

From Bleak Future to Some Sign of Hopes

The Muslim world is in a miserable stage of development, and human misery is everywhere whether in Iraq where people are dying in pain or in Afghanistan where the human suffering has reached unacceptable level or lately in Palestine where the Muslims in Gaza are starved to death while the civilized world is watching the game. Indeed, soaring food prices have worsened the situation, and in the coming months or years we will see civil wars in different parts of the MW and social unrest spread that makes even affluent economies unsafe. No doubt if there is no social justice, there is no peace and prosperity.

Some might argue that man is responsible for the social evils and the environmental destruction and environmental changes under the name of so-called economic development because he has exceeded the limits. This applies not only for individuals but also for corporations that rule the world today, according to a well known journalist John Pilger.

In Islam, an individual is seen as an integral part of the totality of mankind, emphasizing the two-way relationship between the individual and the society. Similarly, to Islamic finance and society, each complements each other; and we cannot separate one from the others. Sadly what we have seen for the last three decades are only investments in mega buildings in different parts of the MW especially affluent economies and expensive hotels (hardware), short-term financing, and less investment in human development resources. Islam focuses on the development of human beings because man is considered to be the vicegerent and active engine for changes in the society.

That has led the managing director and publisher of Islamic Finance News (*www.islamicfinancenews*) to ask this question to scholars in Islamic finance: "With the sovereign wealth funds debate continuing, what role you envisage them playing in the development of the global Islamic finance industry?"

This critical question reflect that due to soaring oil prices enormous cash piles generated that lead huge fund are waving of investing in Wall Street banks following the sub prime crisis in side of investment in human capital in the Muslim world to ease the human suffering in Asia, Africa, and Middle East. At individual or community level and in order to fight poverty and inequality in order to achieve distribution of wealth and income.

Allah says in the Quran: "And those in whose wealth is a recognized right. For the (needy) who asks and him who prevented (For one reason from asking), And those who To the truth of the Day of Judgment, And those who fear the displeasure of their lord. (Sura Maarij 24-27).

This Sura demonstrates that true charity consists in finding out those in real need, whether they ask or not. It is the right of the poor in the wealth of the rich. At the same time the man with wealth or talent or opportunity has the further responsibility of searching out those in need of his assistance, in order to show that he holds all gifts in trust for the service of his fellow creatures.

Qatar the New Direction:
Islamic Finance with Social Responsibility

It is hard for me as researcher in Islamic finance with social responsibility, a new field that I am promoting in the information age after more than twenty-six years of practical and academic experiences to evaluate one country in short time. It requires time and hard work that start from data collection as primary and secondary sources and analyze them to assess critically whether a small nation is a success story or not.

But relatively speaking, I can say Qatar has made a positive impact in the Arab country as well as the Muslim world that needs to be recorded in our modern Islamic history book, which needs to be appreciated. Indeed, her leadership neutrality role in any Arab issues that started from Lebanon and Yemen has made this country well respected not only in the Arab world but far beyond. Thanks to its leadership that is the driving force for economic development with long-term vision, the emir Sheik Hamad bin Khalifa Al-Thani and his wife Her Highness Sheikha Mozah Bint Nasser Al-Missned, the chairperson of Qatar Foundation for Education, Science, and Community Development.

Investment in human capital has made that country in the Arab Gulf focus on global media attention that starts from Aljazeera Arab channel and ends in Aljazeera International Channel in Doha, Kuala Lumpur, and Washington. Once more it is the leadership wisdom to allocate large sum of their oil and gas revenue in R&D investment and attract many Arab scientists and non-Arabs to do research and development. The Doha debates funded by the Qatar Foundation handled by Tim Sebastian, whom readers will remember as the toughest interviewer on television when he hosted the BBC World program HARDtalk, the debates not only present opposing views on some of the hottest topics and Muslim world but also encourage the audience to question both sides.

Qatar leadership needs to give more emphasis on "hands-on experience," and vocational training institution is the answer for youth unemployment in the country. What we have seen in the MW today is that many academic institutions produce unemployable graduates that are big burdens of the government because most courses mainly focus on theories most of which are inapplicable in real life. Qatar today is keen to further diversify her economies away from oil and gas, then investment in agriculture is the answer. It is worth perusing to internationalize her role as she is a caring and sharing nation that looks after the human beings, but the investment should be in human capital; that's what Islamic finance with social responsibility is all about.

In doing so, Qatar can invest in Sudan, Tunisia, and Morocco and ease the financial pressure on these economies. Today there is a food crisis and demands rice plantation, and farming has huge potentials, then QY can learn how to start to learn how to grow rice plantation and rural farming skills that will equip them to be active business partners with their own government that welcomes any new innovative business ideas.

Here the government of Qatar can contact the following institutions: International Rice Research Institute in Manila, Philippines (*www.training.irri.org*), and Telford Rural Polytechnic in New Zealand (*www.telford.ac.nz*), seeking their assistance in this highly demanded area of expertise, as it has been mentioned in chapter 3.

At the end, it is a challenging time for the Muslim world, and we as Muslims in this planet have moral duty and responsibility to open our minds and heart to understand and appreciate the human suffering everywhere in Asia, Africa and Middle East. The Muslim world has to create leaders, not followers, to lead rather than to be led by others and to solve our problem internally not to put their blame on others. Surely the government of Qatar can take this new opportunity to serve this *Ummah* of Islam with Islamic finance with social responsibility.

Qatari success stories in economic and media arenas are well documented and highly respected. Qatar is a small nation with big ideas; it deserves to be the role model for the rest of the Muslim world. Undoubtedly, the banking penetration in the country has been increasing over the last few years. The ratio of credit deployment to gross domestic product (GDP) for Qatar has grown to 49.6 percent at the end of 2006 from 42.8 percent at end of 2004, and in 2007 it is estimated to have reached 69.1 percent mainly because of slowdown in the growth rate of GDP. Such record achievement in the banking industry has translated to the growing importance of Islamic finance, especially in the Gulf Cooperation Council (GCC) region, and has encouraged many Qatari banks to venture into Islamic banking as a window within the conventional bank; but the challenge is not having too many windows with the traditional banking but what Qatar can offer to others in pain some of whom have innovative business ideas but lack finance. It is here where Qatar should promote in the coming months that are Islamic finance with social responsibility to position her that she is a good player in the field.

The Muslim world is indeed looking for new leaders that serve the people and wider communities and understand their needs and wants. That's what Islam is all about as a way of life in order to ease the human suffering in Asia, Africa, and Middle East far beyond Qatari boundary. That's what the author of this book is looking for to make Islamic finance with social responsibility a reality so humanity from wars and poverty and hunger can live in peace.

REFERENCES

Abuzant, Nour (2008): Match skills with job demand, summit told, *www.gulf-times.com*

Al-Harran, S (1999) *New Strategic Alliances between Islamic Financial Institutions, International University Students and Entrepreneurs to Implement Musharakah Financing to Meet the Challenges of the 21ˢᵗ Century*, Arab Law Quarterly, Vol. 14, Part 3 (Special Issue).

Al-Harran, S (2004*) For Today's Social Ills: Islam is the Solution*, A. S. Noordeen, Kuala Lumpur, Malaysia, p. 8.

Al-Harran, S (2006) *How can we turn Brunei into a nation of new ideas?* and *Brunei's main source of new ideas*, Borneo Bulletin, 17 and 18 August.

Al-Harran, S (2008) *Why Strategic Alliances with New Zealand is important for Brunei Darussalam in Managing her Halal Hub and far beyond into the future.* Paper presented at the International Conference on Business and Management on *Creating Competitive Advantage in the Global Economy*, Organized by the Faculty of Business, Economics and Policy Studies, Universiti Brunei Darussalam (UBD), 8-9 January 2008.

Al-Harran, S, Alfred Yong Foh Sen and Anne Masri (2008) *An Islamic Microfinance Enterprise, The Financial Vehicle that Will Change the Face of the Muslim World*, Xlibris Corporation, USA.

Al-Rashed, M A (2006) *Bawareq of Iraq*, Dar AlUmmah, pp. 46-47.

Anjum, U, (2007) *Cooperation: The Qur'anic Imperative: Reaching Out to Humanity for Charity and Piety*, Al-Jumuah, vol. 19, issue 08.

Asia Inc (2007) "The Brunei Growth Story: Brunei Premium Halal Brand," July-August, p. 82.

Borneo Bulletin, 17 August 2006, Brunei Darussalam.

Borneo Bulletin, 18 August 2006, Brunei Darussalam.

Burgmann T. (2007) "Halal flexes its marketing muscle," *The Star*, 22 July.

Canterprise (2007) *the arm of Canterbury University, Christchurch,* New Zealand (*www.cant.canterbury.ac.nz*).

Drury, A (2007) "Halal Place in New Zealand," *The Nelson Mail,* 15 September 2007, p. 14.

El-Mouelhy, M. (2007) "Marketing Halal."

Eltahawy, Mona (2006): The Muslim World is Lost at Sea without a Captain, *www.aawsat.com/english/*

Evans, Hj A. "Halal: A New Market Identifier," Excerpts from "Understanding the Muslim Consumers," The Halal Journal in *The Brunei Times,* 17 August 2007, p. 6.

Farouk, M (2006) *New Zealand Muslims: A Conduit for Business in Malaysia.* Paper presented at a one-day seminar on "Islam and the Global Economy Malaysia and New Zealand Perspective" organized by the chair of Malay studies and the School of Marketing and International Business, Victoria University of Wellington, New Zealand.

Global Investment House (2008): Qatar Banking Sector Soars, *www.islamic financenews.com*

Hadthiah PD, H, and Romulo T L (2007) *Brunei's Farm Sector Needs a Short in the Arm,* (*www.brudirect.com/DailyInfo/News/Archive/Sept07/140907/nite18.htm*)

Han, S. (2007) "Halal Brand Eyes First Product by Next Expo," *The Brunei Times,* 20 August 2007, p. 1.

Han, S. (2007 a) "Labelling for Halal Products," *The Brunei Times,* 20 August 2007, p. 5.

Hazair, Hadthiah P. D. (2007) "Aviod Haram Names for Halal Food," *The Brunei Times*, 19

Hazair, Hadthiah P. D. (2007a) "More Trade Than Halal Seal," *The Brunei Times*, 21 August 2007, p. 13.

Hazair, Hadthiah P.D. (2007b) "Nestle interested in obtaining Brunei Halal Seal," *The Brunei Times*, 20 August 2007, p. 13.

Hazair, Hadthiah P. D (2007c) "Branding Key to Makining Halal Goods Click," *The Brunei Times*, 26 August 2007, p. 8.

Ida W, (2007) *Aiming to be a global player in the Premium Halal Market, Asia Inc* July-August.

Imady O and Hans Dieter Seible, www.manara.in/res.html.

Izam S and Shareen Han (2007) *Australian firm may tie-up with Brunei for halal brand*, The Brunei Times, 25 September.

Lendrum, T. (1998). *The Strategic Partnering Handbook*, 6-7.

Low Kim Cheng, Patrick and Al-Harran, S (2007) *Negotiating Your Way: The Islamic way, lecture Notes*, Faculty of Business, Economics and Policy Studies, UBD.

Low Kim Cheng, P. (2007) "A Kazakhstan Perspective on Diversity," *The Asian Journal of Organizational Behavior*, January, p. 18-32.

Marta Steeman, (2007) *From Good Ideas to the Market, The Press*, Christchurch, 15 September.

Statistics New Zealand Web site
The Canterbury Community Trust (2007)
(*www.commtrust.org.nz*)

Telford Rural Polytechnic, Booklet, *www.telford.ac.nz www.newzealandnow.info www.nzedge.com/heroes/hillary.html www.newzealandbeef.org*

Theompson, A. A. and Stirckland, A. J. (1995), *Strategic Management, Concept and Cases*, 8th edition, 155-167.

The Brunei Times, (2008) Islamic banking to keep growing: Moody's, 27 February.

The Straits Times (2007) *Editorial Review,* Singapore 4 October, p. 26.

The Sunday Herald (Scotland) 2008: "The year of global food crisis," 9 March. August 2007, p. 8.

Varina N, (2006) *Challenging your thinking,* Manpower Australia (*www.manpower. com.au*).

Yusuf, A, (1983) The Holy Quran: Text, Translation and Commentary.

Yussof A, *(2007) Youth unemployment among the graduate is serious concern in the mind of the government? How can we resolve this problem? Is there a way out?* Unpublished paper, CIBFM, UBD.

INDEX

A

advertising, 34
Aljazeera, 45, 50, 55

B

branding, 33
Brunei, 10, 21
  as strategic partner of New Zealand, 17
  economy, 12
  government, 13, 16, 36, 39
  on halal business, 16
  population, 12
Brunei Premium Halal Brand, 16
Brunei Youth Venture Capital
    Company, 41
BYVCC. *See* Brunei Youth Venture
    Capital Company; *See* Brunei
    Youth Venture Capital
    Company

C

Canterbury University, 18, 46
Canterprise, 18, 46
China, 2, 29
Christchurch Polytechnic Institute of
    Technology, 17, 55

collaboration, 8, 9, 44
competition, 16
cooperation, 8, 9, 12, 20, 44, 58

E

ecotourism, 19

F

faith, 58, 60
Federation of Islamic Associations of New
    Zealand, 15
FIANZ. *See* Federation of Islamic
    Associations of New Zealand; *See*
    Federation of Islamic Associations
    of New Zealand

H

halal
  beef, 15
  certification, 15, 32, 35
  market, 15, 16, 31
  product industry, 3
  sheep meat, 15

PHOTOS OF PUBLISHED BOOKS

BY DR. SAAD AL-HARRAN

AN ISLAMIC MICROFINANCE ENTERPRISE

THE FINANCIAL VEHICLE
THAT WILL CHANGE THE FACE
OF THE ISLAMIC WORLD

THE POWER OF SALAM FINANCING

BY
DR. SAAD AL-HARRAN
AND
ALFRED YONG FOH SEN   SRI ANNE HAJI MASRI

**Leading
Issues in**

Islamic
Banking
and
Finance

Edited by
DR. SAAD AL-HARRAN

PELANDUK PUBLICATIONS

www.ingramcontent.com/pod-product-compliance
Lightning Source LLC
Chambersburg PA
CBHW022111170526
45157CB00004B/1586